ON THE PITCH
PITCH

MASTERING THE SKILLS

BY
TOBY RIVERS

© 2024, Digital Craft Publishing

All rights reserved. Apart from any fair dealing for the purposes of private study, research, criticism, or review, as permitted under the Copyright Act 1968, no part of this publication may be reproduced, stored in a retrieval system, or transmitted in any form or by any means, electronic, mechanical, photocopying, recording, or otherwise, without prior written permission from the copyright owner.

Any unauthorised commercial use of this publication or its contents is strictly prohibited. The moral rights of the author have been asserted.

First published in 2024 in Australia.

ISBN : 978-1-7637778-2-8

All correspondence to: info@digitalcraftpublishing.com

www.digialcraftpublishing.com

"Success is no accident. It is hard work, perseverance, learning, studying, sacrifice, and most of all, love of what you are doing or learning to do."

Pele

Main Characters

Robin is an 11-year-old Australian boy with straight brown hair, slightly shorter than his peers, and often seen wearing worn soccer gear. Determined and passionate, Robin grows from a quiet and unsure player into a confident leader on the field. His greatest strength is his vision, allowing him to see plays unfold before they happen, making him a natural playmaker. Through his journey, Robin learns that soccer is not just about winning, but about teamwork, inclusion, and the joy of the game.

Jake is Robin's close friend and teammate, known for his messy brown hair and quick, athletic build. His energy and positivity are contagious, and he always cheers on his teammates and especially supports Robin's growth. As a winger, Jake's speed and timing make him a key player in executing Robin's brilliant passes. His enthusiasm for the game and friendly nature help bring the team together, making him an essential part of the group.

Callum is tall and strong, has dark hair, and has a competitive nature. Initially, Callum is aggressive and focused on winning at all costs, but over time, he grows to appreciate teamwork and respect Robin's leadership. Though sceptical of new players at first, Callum learns to value the inclusiveness that Robin fosters. As a versatile player, Callum's defensive and attacking abilities make him a formidable presence on the field.

Dylan is the team's quiet and composed defensive back, with blond hair, blue eyes, and long legs that help him cover ground quickly. He is thoughtful and strategic, rarely speaking but always observing and staying one step ahead of opponents. Dylan shares a mutual respect with Robin, appreciating the technical side of the game. His calm demeanour under pressure and strong positioning make him a reliable defender for the team.

Leo is the tall, lean goalkeeper with sandy blond hair and sharp green eyes, known for his quick reflexes and focus. Though he faces Robin's set pieces and powerful shots, Leo respects Robin's skill and growth. Competitive yet fair, Leo challenges Robin during critical moments of the game but ultimately shares the same values of respect and teamwork, recognizing the importance of playing with integrity.

Mason is the 16-year-old mentor who has been crucial in Robin's development. With messy, curly dark hair, tan skin, and quiet confidence, Mason was once an underdog in soccer himself. He recognizes Robin's potential early on and helps him develop his skills, focusing on passing, ball control, and vision. Mason's calm, patient teaching style has shaped Robin into the player he is, and his wisdom about the game's deeper meaning—respect, teamwork, and enjoyment—stays with Robin throughout his journey.

Contents

The Love of the Game 1

A New Game, A New Place 6

Words of Wisdom 11

Meet the Mentor 15

Dribble Like a Pro 21

The Showdown 26

Shooting for Success 31

The Big Match 36

The Perfect Pass 41

Passing with Purpose 46

The Final Tackle 51

Defending the Dream 56

Mastering the Midfield 61

Being in the Right Time at the Right Place 65

Speed and Agility 70

Quick Turns, Sharp Reactions 76

More Than Just Soccer 81

Mastering the Touch 84

The Ball Control Battle 89

The Playmaker's Vision 94

Visionary Playmaking 98

Crossing the Line 103

The Ultimate Passing Test 108

Set Pieces, Big Moments 113

Taking the Free Kick 118

Sportsmanship Above All 122

The Ultimate Test 126

A New Beginning 131

The Love of the Game

Passion
True passion isn't about winning; it's about the joy of playing every game with heart. Let your love for the game fuel every step.

The sun set over the neighbourhood field, casting long shadows on the worn-out grass. The ball rolled at Robin's feet, barging as he struggled to keep it under control. He wasn't the best player, but his love for soccer ran deep. Every afternoon after school, no matter how tired he felt or how badly he played, he was always out on the field.

Robin was an 11-year-old boy, a bit shorter than most of his friends, with straight brown hair that often fell over his forehead in messy strands as he ran. His skin was sun-kissed from hours spent playing outside, with freckles scattered across his cheeks and nose. His eyes, a soft hazel, always seemed to hold a quiet determination. He wore a faded soccer jersey, his favourite, though it was a bit too big for him—probably a hand-me-down from his dad. His soccer boots were scuffed, with the laces frayed from use, but they fit him perfectly, like an old friend that had seen many games. The knees of his shorts were stained from sliding tackles, a testament to the many hours he spent on the field. "Come on, Robin, give it a proper kick!" his friend called, waving from the goalpost. Robin narrowed his eyes, focused, and swung his foot towards the ball. But instead of soaring into the goal, it veered wildly to the left, bouncing into the bushes.

"Nice try!" his best friend shouted with a laugh. Robin smiled weakly, trying to laugh it off, but inside, it stung. He wanted to be good. No—he wanted to be great. But the reality was that he wasn't. Not yet, at least.

Robin had always been quiet, more of a thinker than a talker, but he was relentless in his pursuit of improvement. While his friends would laugh and joke, Robin often stayed behind after the games, pushing himself harder, trying to master the elusive control he saw in professional players. Every missed shot, every fumbled touch, only made him more determined. His slight frame didn't give him an advantage in size, but he had quick feet and sharp instincts—skills he knew would improve with time.

As the last game of the evening wrapped up, Robin stayed behind, kicking the ball around on his own. He constantly watched the professional players on TV and wondered how they made it look effortless. At his feet, the ball seemed to have a mind. Still, he practised whenever possible, even if no one was watching.

At home, soccer was everything. His dad, once a decent player himself, always encouraged him to keep going. "The best players didn't start out as the best," his dad would say, clapping him on the shoulder after another brutal practice and adding, "How hard you work when no one's watching makes the difference."

Robin's neighbourhood was small and quiet, a close-knit community where everyone knew each other. The streets were lined with simple houses, their gardens well-kept, and the local park with the soccer field was a hub of activity for the kids. The field itself was far from perfect—patches of grass were worn down to dirt, and the goalposts were rusty—but for Robin, it was a place of comfort. Here, he felt a sense of freedom, away from school and the pressures of fitting in. It was just him, the ball, and the game he loved.

His mum was always his biggest supporter, too. "You'll get there, Robin," she'd tell him at the end of every match, no matter how badly it had gone. "It just takes time, love."

Soccer wasn't just a hobby for Robin; it was a way to connect with something bigger, maybe even a way to connect with his dad. When he played, all the frustrations and worries faded, replaced by the simple focus of kicking the ball, aiming for a goal that felt both far away and within reach. Soccer helped him tune out everything else, like the constant doubt that gnawed at him—was he ever going to be good enough?

Robin sensed something different as he stepped into the kitchen that evening, still wiping sweat from his brow.

His parents were sitting at the table, their faces unusually serious. His dad looked up and forced a smile.

"Hey, mate. Come and sit down. We've got something to talk about."

Robin's stomach sank. He dropped his ball by the door and sat at the table. "What's wrong?" he asked, glancing between his parents.

His dad cleared his throat. "We're moving," he said quietly. "I've got a new job, which means we'll leave the neighbourhood next month."

Robin's world seemed to tilt. "Moving? But... where?" His voice cracked.

"To a new suburb. It's not too far," his dad explained, "but it'll be a fresh start for all of us."

Robin sat back, the words settling in. The field he practised on every day, the friends he played with—he'd be leaving it all behind. "I... I don't want to move," he muttered, staring at the table. "What about soccer? What about my friends?"

His mum leaned forward, resting her hand on his. "You'll make new friends, Robin. And there'll be other places to play soccer, I'm sure. Maybe you'll even find a team that can help you improve."

Robin looked up at her, doubt clouding his mind. "But what if the kids there are even better than the ones here? What if they... laugh at me?"

His dad leaned forward. "I know it's scary, son. But moving doesn't mean you stop playing. You've worked hard and get better no matter where we are."

Robin didn't respond. He just nodded, excusing himself from the table. "I'm going to bed."

He walked towards his room, his parents' voices fading behind him as he closed the door. In the dim light of his bedroom, he sat on the edge of the bed and picked up his soccer ball, rolling it between his hands.

He wasn't ready for what was coming, but he knew one thing: he couldn't stop playing. Soccer was still everything.

A New Game, A New Place

Adaptability
Change is a new field to conquer; embrace it with open arms and watch yourself grow in unexpected ways.

Robin watched silently as the moving van pulled away, leaving behind stacks of boxes in the new house. The place was excellent, he supposed. It is more significant than their old home, with a neat garden out front and plenty of space inside. But to Robin, it didn't feel right. Not yet.

The houses were pristine and larger than what Robin was used to. The sidewalks here were perfectly paved, with no cracks or familiar markings like the ones back home where he and his friends had carved their initials. He kicked his soccer ball lightly with his foot as he stood in the driveway, glancing up and down the unfamiliar street. The roads felt too wide, like they stretched on without end, making him feel smaller than he ever did in his old neighbourhood. The houses looked different, the roads wider, and everything felt too clean, like it didn't belong to him. The friends, the games, the familiar fields he had left behind – they all seemed so far away now.

"Why don't you go explore the park?" his dad called from the front door, carrying another box inside. "There's supposed to be a soccer pitch nearby. Could be fun to see what the neighbourhood's like."

Robin nodded, more out of habit than enthusiasm, and walked down the street with his ball under his arm. As he walked, his mind wandered to the old soccer field he used to play on. It wasn't much—just some dirt patches and rusted goalposts—but it had character. It was theirs. Here, everything looked perfect, untouched. Too clean. He found the park after a few minutes—a vast green space with a proper soccer pitch. A group of kids were already there, kicking a ball around in the distance.

For a second, excitement flickered in Robin's chest. Maybe this could be his chance to make new friends and fit in. But as he got closer, the excitement twisted into nervousness. The grass on the field looked flawless, trimmed perfectly with bright white lines marking the boundaries, nothing like the worn-out patches and faded lines he was used to. These kids weren't like the ones back home. They were fast, passing the ball precisely, dribbling quickly past each other. Robin's stomach dropped. They were really good.

Still, he had to try.

Clutching the ball tighter, he approached them cautiously, stopping just outside the pitch. He stood there for a moment, watching them play. They hadn't noticed him yet. His heart thudded in his chest. He didn't want to make the first move, but what choice did he have?

"Hey, can I join?"

The group stopped playing and turned to look at him. Robin suddenly felt very small. The pitch that had seemed inviting just moments ago now felt overwhelming. The tallest boy, clearly the leader, glanced at Robin's ball, then back at him. He smirked.

"Sure, new kid. Let's see what you've got."

Robin hesitated. Something in the boy's tone made him uneasy, but he stepped onto the pitch anyway, trying to hide the nervous knot in his stomach. He took a deep breath, waiting for the ball to come.

It didn't take long for the first pass to head his way. Robin reached for it with his foot, but the ball slipped past him. He chased after it awkwardly, but by the time he'd caught up, one of the other boys had already swooped in to take it away.

Laughter rippled through the group. "What was that?" the leader called out, his smirk widening. "Can't you even control the ball?"

Robin's cheeks burned, but he stayed quiet. He needed another chance, another pass. This time, he'd get it right.

But the game continued, and every time the ball came near him, it was the same. He couldn't keep up with their quick passes, missed his shots, and every mistake was met with more laughter. Robin could feel his heart sinking lower with each failure, the weight of the humiliation heavy on his shoulders. The leader, whose name Robin had learned was Callum, seemed to find each misstep funnier than the last.

"Maybe soccer isn't your thing, new kid," Callum said with a grin. "Might want to try something easier, like… chess."

The others laughed, and Robin's face burned with humiliation. His heart was pounding in his ears, the sting of their words hitting harder than any missed pass. He clenched his fists, fighting back the tears that threatened to spill. He wanted to disappear, to walk away and never come back.

"I've had enough," Robin muttered, stepping away from the group. He could still hear them laughing as he walked off the pitch, shoulders hunched and eyes focused on the ground before him.

As he walked, he kicked his soccer ball lightly, but each kick felt heavier than the last. The joy he'd felt at seeing the park was gone, replaced with a heavy knot in his chest. He didn't belong here.

When he got home, the house was quieter. His parents were still busy unpacking, so he slipped into his room, hoping no one would notice how badly the afternoon had gone.

At dinner, though, his mum was quick to ask. "How was it at the park, love? Did you meet anyone?"

Robin poked at his food, not meeting her eyes. "It was fine," he said quickly, not wanting to talk about it.

"Did you play a game?" his dad asked. "You'll make friends in no time, Robin. Just give it a little time."

Robin gave a slight nod, forcing a smile that didn't reach his eyes. "Yeah. I'll give it time."

But as he lay in bed that night, staring up at the ceiling, he wasn't sure time would be enough. Those kids were good—much better than him. He wasn't ready for this. He wasn't prepared for any of it.

Words of Wisdom

Insight
Every lesson is a gift—take it to heart, for wisdom is the greatest guide on your journey.

The next few days were a blur for Robin. He avoided the park and the soccer pitch, not wanting to face Callum and the others again. The humiliation of being laughed at still stung, and every time he thought about going back, his stomach twisted in knots. He kept to himself at home, kicking his ball lightly around the backyard, but it didn't feel the same. His heart wasn't in it anymore.

It wasn't long before his dad noticed something was off. One evening, after dinner, his dad knocked on the door to Robin's room and stepped inside.

"You all right, Robin?"

Robin sat on his bed, staring at the soccer ball in his hands. "Yeah, I'm fine," he muttered, not looking up. He didn't want to talk about what had happened, but he knew his dad could tell something was wrong.

His dad sat down at the foot of the bed, giving Robin a moment before speaking again. "You sure? You've been pretty quiet lately. Haven't seen you at the park."

Robin shrugged, trying to brush it off, but the words spilt out before he could stop them. "It's just… the kids at the park. They're all so good. Way better than me. I tried to play with them, but I messed up. A lot." He glanced up, catching his dad's eyes for a moment. "They laughed at me, Dad. I couldn't even control the ball, and they just laughed."

His dad nodded, listening patiently. "That must've felt pretty rough."

Robin nodded, his face heating up as he remembered Callum's mocking grin and the laughter from the other kids. "I just… I don't know. I'm never going to be as good as them. What's the point if I'm always going to mess up?"

There was a silence for a moment, and Robin's dad sighed. "Robin, I know that feeling all too well. When I was your age, I went through the same thing. I loved soccer, but I wasn't great at it. I remember joining a local team and thinking I could keep up, but when the games started, I kept making mistakes. I was embarrassed, frustrated… felt like giving up."

Robin looked at him, surprised. "You? But you were good."

His dad chuckled. "Not at first. I had to work for it. And there were plenty of times when I thought about quitting. But that's the thing about soccer—or anything, really. You're not going to be great right away. No one is. Even the best players have had their fair share of failures."

Robin frowned, looking back down at his soccer ball. "But what if I never get better? What if I keep messing up, and they never let me play with them again?"

His dad leaned forward. "Robin, what matters isn't how good you are right now. It's about how hard you're willing to work to get better. Every player starts somewhere. The difference between the ones who succeed and those who don't is that the ones who succeed don't give up, no matter how many times they fall."

Robin stayed quiet, thinking over his dad's words. It was hard to imagine himself ever being as good as Callum and the others. But he also knew he couldn't just sit around feeling sorry for himself. That wouldn't change anything.

"I know it's tough," his dad continued. "But here's the thing—if you give up now, you'll never know how much you could've improved. But if you keep practising and working on your game, you'll get better little by little. It's not going to happen overnight, but it will happen. And one day, you'll look back and see how far you've come."

Robin sighed. "It just feels like I'm so far behind."

"You're not, though," his dad said, shaking his head. "You've got the most important part already—your love for the game. That's what's going to push you through the tough times. As long as you don't give up, you'll get there. I know it."

Robin was quiet for a long time, his dad's words swirling around in his mind. He still felt the sting of the laughter and the embarrassment of messing up, but there was something else there now—a tiny flicker of hope. Maybe his dad was right. Perhaps he wasn't good enough yet, but that didn't mean he never would be.

His dad stood up and smiled. "Take it one step at a time, Robin. You've got this." He gave him a pat on the shoulder before heading out of the room.

Robin sat there for a while, staring at the soccer ball in his hands. His dad's words played over and over in his mind: *What matters isn't how good you are now. It's about how hard you're willing to work.*

Slowly, Robin stood up and placed the ball on the floor. He kicked it lightly, feeling its familiar weight under his foot. He wasn't sure how long it would take or how many times he'd mess up again. But one thing was sure: he wasn't ready to give up.

Meet the Mentor

Guidance
A mentor's belief can light the way forward. Trust their guidance as you shape your path.

The following day, Robin woke up determined. He wasn't ready to quit. His dad's words had stuck with him: *It's not how good you are now; it's how hard you're willing to work.* With his soccer ball in hand, Robin made his way to the park, aiming to practice by himself. He found a quiet spot by a wall and began kicking the ball, trying to improve his control without the pressure of other people watching.

As he focused on his kicks, a voice interrupted him from behind.

"You're too stiff with your dribbles."

Robin spun around to see a boy slightly older than him standing a few feet away. The boy looked about 16 years old, with messy, curly dark hair that hung over his forehead, his tan skin covered in patches of dried dirt as if he had already spent hours playing. He wore a worn-out jersey with faded colours and slightly torn shorts—soccer had clearly been a major part of his day. But what stood out most were his eyes: sharp, focused, and filled with quiet confidence. He had a soccer ball tucked under his arm and watched Robin with a raised eyebrow. His casual confidence threw Robin off.

"What?" Robin asked, frowning.

"You're concentrating too much on the ball," the boy repeated. "You're supposed to feel it, not force it. Loosen up."

Robin stood there, unsure how to respond. He didn't even know this kid, yet here he was offering advice. Robin hesitated but then nodded slightly. "Okay, how do you know that?"

The boy smirked, a hint of amusement in his expression. "I've been where you are—stiff, awkward, trying too hard. But I had someone show me the right way to play." He paused, his face softening. "You remind me of how I started." Without waiting for Robin's response, the boy dropped his ball and began dribbling. His movements were fluid as if the ball was part of him. He moved without effort, keeping his head up, feet light, and the ball always within his control.

Robin's jaw dropped. He hadn't seen anyone move like that in person before.

"How did you learn to do that?" Robin asked, unable to hide the awe in his voice.

The boy stopped and grinned. "Years of practice. But not just any practice—smart practice. Many kids think kicking a ball around is enough, but that's not how you improve."

Robin looked down at his own ball, kicking it lightly. "I've been practising too, but... I'm just not good enough."

The boy studied him for a moment, a serious expression replacing his grin. "I've seen plenty of kids give up because they didn't think they had what it takes. But the only difference between the ones who get better and the ones who don't is the willingness to keep going, even when it's tough." He paused, then added, "The question is, do you want to get better, or are you just hoping it'll get easier on its own?"

The boy looked at Robin carefully, reading his expression. "So what? You think you can't get better?"

Robin shrugged. "I don't know. The kids at the park—they're way better than me. Every time I try, I mess up. I want to be good, but I don't know where to start."

The boy crossed his arms, still holding his soccer ball. "Why do you even want to be good?"

Robin blinked, surprised by the question. "What do you mean?"

"Why are you doing this? If you're not good now, why bother?"

Robin hesitated, thinking about his answer. "Because… I love soccer, even if I'm not good at it. I just… I want to be better. I don't want to be the kid everyone laughs at."

The boy stayed quiet for a moment, his gaze steady. Robin noticed a flicker of something in the boy's expression—understanding, maybe even a bit of sympathy. "You're serious about this, huh?"

Robin nodded. "Yeah, I am. I don't want to quit just because it's hard."

The boy seemed to mull this over, his gaze drifting toward the soccer ball Robin held. After a few seconds, he spoke again. "I used to be like you, you know—always the kid getting picked last, messing up all the time. It sucked. But someone helped me once. Showed me what it took to get better." He paused, his voice lowering slightly. "And now, I can't stand to see someone like you give up when they haven't even started yet. That's why I'm willing to help."

The boy took a deep breath, his expression softening slightly. "All right, I get it. Look, it's not easy. Everyone starts out bad. But if you're serious—and I mean serious—I can help you. I can show you a few things, but it will take much work."

Robin's heart lifted, but he didn't let himself get too excited yet. "You think I can get better?"

The boy tilted his head. "It depends. Are you willing to listen and put in the time?"

Robin nodded quickly. "Yeah. I'll do whatever it takes."

The boy finally smiled. "All right then. I'm Mason, by the way."

"Robin."

"Good to meet you, Robin. Let's start with your dribbling. I saw what you were doing, and we need to fix your touch."

Mason placed the ball before Robin and showed him a simple drill. "Keep the ball close, but don't keep staring at it. You have to feel where it is. Pretend it's tied to your feet."

Robin tried to follow Mason's instructions. At first, it was difficult—his movements were too stiff, and the ball kept slipping away. But Mason was patient, giving him pointers and correcting his technique.

"Relax," Mason said after one of Robin's attempts. "You're too tense. Soccer's about rhythm. You've got to move with the ball, not against it."

Slowly, Robin began to understand. His movements became smoother, the ball staying closer to his feet. He wasn't perfect, but for the first time, he felt he was improving, even a little.

After about an hour, Robin was exhausted, but he also felt a flicker of hope. Mason's guidance had given him something to work with—something concrete to focus on.

As they wrapped up, Robin looked at Mason gratefully. "Thanks for helping me. I didn't think anyone would take the time."

Mason shrugged, wiping sweat from his forehead. "I've been there. You just need someone to push you in the right direction." He paused, giving Robin a serious look. "But don't think this is it. You've got a long way to go, and I'm not going to be around all the time. You have to put in the work when no one's watching."

Robin nodded. "I'll keep working."

Mason looked at him for a moment before nodding. "All right then. I'll see you around. Keep practising those drills, and maybe I'll give you more tips later."

Robin smiled. "I will."

As he walked home, the knot of doubt in his chest loosened a bit. Mason hadn't promised anything, but the fact that he was willing to help meant something. Maybe, just maybe, he could get better.

Dribble Like a Pro

Skill

Great skill is built with patience and practice; let each dribble bring you closer to mastery.

Robin arrived at the park early, feeling a mix of determination and nervous energy. He had been practising the drills Mason had shown him, but today was different. He was meeting Mason again and wanted to prove he had been working hard. His soccer ball was tucked under his arm as he scanned the field for his mentor.

Mason appeared a few minutes later, casually dribbling a ball towards him. "Ready to work?" Mason asked, his usual calm, confident smile in place.

Robin nodded. "Yeah, I've been practising the drills."

Mason gave a slight approving nod. "Good. But today, we're going to take it deeper. You're getting better at controlling the ball, but you must understand why dribbling matters."

Robin looked up, curious. He knew dribbling was important, but this was the first time anyone explained it to him.

Mason stood still momentarily, letting the silence sink in before speaking. "Dribbling isn't just about getting past defenders. It's about control—of the ball, the field, and the game. The best players are the ones who can keep possession, no matter what. When you can dribble well, you don't lose the ball easily and don't rely on someone else to create the play for you."

Robin watched closely as Mason placed the ball at his feet, moving it smoothly from side to side. His touch was light, almost effortless. "When you're dribbling, it's not just about showing off or doing tricks. It's about keeping the ball close to you, always knowing where it is. If you can control the ball, you can control the game."

Robin nodded slowly. "But how do I get that kind of control?"

"That's where practice comes in," Mason said, his eyes locking on Robin's. "Many kids think they can kick the ball and magically get better. But that's not how it works. You must focus on the basics—close control, light touches, and keeping your head up. Dribbling isn't just about what your feet are doing. It's about seeing the field, feeling the ball, and knowing your next move before you make it."

Mason set up a line of cones in front of Robin. "We'll start with something simple. Dribbling between these cones will help you get comfortable with the ball at your feet. But remember, don't rush. This isn't about speed—it's about control."

Robin began weaving the ball between the cones, but his movements were stiff, and the ball slipped away from him more than once. He gritted his teeth, trying to push through the frustration.

Mason watched quietly for a while before stepping in. "You're too tense, Robin. Loosen up. You're trying to force the ball to do what you want. Instead, you need to guide it."

Robin stopped, panting lightly. "Guide it?"

Mason nodded. "Dribbling is like a dance. The ball is your partner, but you're leading. You don't yank it around; you move with it. Keep your touches light, and keep the ball close. Let me show you again."

Mason demonstrated, weaving through the cones with smooth, controlled touches. His feet barely seemed to touch the ball, but the ball responded perfectly to every move.

"See?" Mason said, looking up. "Small, controlled touches. Keep the ball close, and always be ready to change direction. Now, you try."

Robin took a deep breath and started again. This time, he focused on keeping his touches light, just like Mason had shown him. Slowly, the ball began to stay closer to his feet. It wasn't perfect, but it was better than before.

"That's it," Mason said, nodding as Robin made his way through the cones. "You're getting there. Keep practising that, and it'll start to feel more natural."

After a few more runs through the cones, Mason moved on to the next drill. "All right, let's talk about shielding. In a game, you're not always going to have space. Defenders will be all over you, trying to take the ball away. When that happens, you need to know how to protect it."

Mason demonstrated how to use his body to shield the ball, keeping his arms out and his back turned to the imaginary defender. "The key is to keep your body between the ball and the defender. Don't let them get close enough to make a tackle. You're in control, not them."

Robin tried the drill, using his body to block an invisible opponent while moving the ball forward. It was more complicated than it looked, but after a few tries, he started to get the hang of it.

"Good," Mason said, giving him a small smile. "You're learning fast."

As they continued, Mason showed Robin a few dribbling moves to help him in one-on-one situations. "If you're up against a defender, you've got to make them think you're going one way, then go the other. It's all about unpredictability."

Mason demonstrated the feint, faking a move in one direction before quickly shifting the ball to the other foot and taking off in the opposite direction. Then he showed

Robin the drag-back, pulling the ball back with the sole of his foot to change direction quickly.

Robin practised the moves, his heart racing with excitement. He had seen other players use these kinds of tricks, but he had never thought he could pull them off. With Mason's guidance, though, he felt like it was possible.

"You're doing great," Mason said as they wrapped up. "Remember, it's not about speed or power. It's about control. When you're dribbling, you decide where the ball goes. Not the defender. Not anyone else. You."

By the end of the session, Robin was exhausted but proud. He could feel the improvement. His touches were lighter, and the ball felt more like a part of him, not something he had to fight.

As they packed up, Mason gave Robin one last piece of advice. "Next time you're out there with Callum and the others, don't focus on beating them with speed. Focus on keeping control. You'll surprise them if you can dribble and keep the ball close."

Robin nodded, his determination growing. He wasn't sure when he would face Callum again, but when the time came, he'd be ready.

The Showdown

Challenge
Challenges are just opportunities to prove your strength. Face them head-on and show what you're made of.

Robin walked to the park, his soccer ball tucked under his arm. The morning sun was bright, and the air was crisp, making him feel more alert. He wasn't sure what would happen today, but he knew one thing—he wasn't the same player who had left the field in shame after Callum's mocking laughter. He had practised hard and was ready to prove he could hold his own.

As he approached the field, he saw Callum and his group playing their usual game. Robin felt his stomach tighten with nerves, but alongside the nerves was a growing sense of determination. He couldn't help but remember the last time he faced these kids—the taunts, the humiliation—but today was different. He wasn't the same player anymore, and he wasn't going to stay on the sidelines.

Robin stepped onto the edge of the field, catching Callum's eye. It didn't take long for the taunts to start.

"Well, well, look who decided to show up again," Callum called out, smirking as he kicked the ball lazily toward one of his friends. "Back for another lesson on how not to play?"

The other kids snickered, but Robin kept his face calm. Instead of feeling embarrassed, he felt a surge of focus. He was ready for this.

"Let me join," Robin said, his voice steady. He didn't ask—he stated it like a challenge.

Callum raised an eyebrow, clearly surprised by Robin's confidence. For a second, a flicker of hesitation crossed his face, but he quickly covered it up with his usual smirk. "You want to join? How about we make it more interesting? One-on-one. Let's see what you've got."

The smirk on Callum's face was all too familiar. He expected to humiliate Robin again, to show how much better he was. But Robin wasn't the same player anymore, and today, Callum was about to find out.

"Fine," Robin agreed, setting his soccer ball down. His heart pounded in his chest, but he kept his breathing steady. He took a deep breath, remembering Mason's advice: keep the ball close, stay calm, and know your next move before you make it.

The other kids circled, eager to watch what they thought would be an easy defeat. Robin could feel their eyes on him, their quiet whispers and chuckles building the tension. But he blocked it all out, focusing only on the ball and the game ahead. Callum stepped forward, confidence radiating off him. "You'll regret this," he said, grinning as he prepared to attack.

The game started, and almost immediately, Callum charged at Robin. For a split second, time seemed to slow. Robin's heart raced, but his mind stayed clear. He kept his eyes forward, just like Mason had taught him, and began dribbling with small, controlled touches, keeping the ball close to his feet.

Callum lunged at him, but Robin sidestepped, using his body to shield the ball. He could hear the gasps from the other kids, their surprise fueling his focus. Callum's frustration grew, and Robin could feel the shift. This wasn't like before. He wasn't flustered or unsure. He knew what he was doing.

"Come on, Robin!" Callum jeered, his voice tinged with annoyance. His smirk faltered, his confidence slipping for the first time. "Is that all you've got?"

Robin didn't respond. Instead, he waited for the right moment, remembering what Mason had said about one-on-one situations. He needed to make Callum think he was going one way, then go the other. His heart pounded, but his mind was clear.

Callum's expression hardened, and Robin could see the tension building in his body language. He was used to being in control, but now Robin was making him work for it. As Callum closed in again, Robin faked a movement to the right—just enough to make Callum commit. Then, with a quick flick, Robin shifted the ball to his left and darted past Callum, executing the feint flawlessly.

The field seemed to freeze. Callum stumbled, caught completely off guard. His eyes widened as Robin darted past him, disbelief flickering across his face. By the time he recovered, Robin was already a few steps ahead, dribbling the ball with control and precision.

The other kids gasped. No one had expected this, least of all Callum. Robin could hear the murmurs of surprise from the sidelines, but he didn't let it distract him. He kept his focus, moving the ball steadily toward the goal.

He took a shot—it wasn't perfect and missed the goal by a small margin—but that didn't matter. The message had been sent: Robin wasn't the same kid they had laughed at before.

Callum's face flushed with frustration. He kicked the ground, trying to hide his embarrassment, but it was clear to everyone that something had changed. He tried to laugh it off, to brush it away with a sarcastic comment, but the tension in his voice betrayed him. "Lucky move," he muttered, though the other kids didn't seem to buy it.

One of the boys from the group, a tall kid named Jake, approached Robin, his expression shifting from disbelief to something closer to respect. "That was a nice move," Jake said, nodding. "Didn't know you had it in you."

Robin felt a small surge of pride at the compliment. He hadn't won the game outright but had earned something more substantial—respect.

Callum, now visibly agitated, kicked the ball back to the centre of the field. His usual confidence had given way to something darker—determination tinged with frustration. "Let's go again," he growled, his eyes narrowing. He wasn't ready to give up control just yet. But this time, things were different.

Shooting for Success

Focus

Focus is your greatest tool. Lock your eyes on the goal and let nothing break your aim.

Robin arrived at the park early again, his confidence building after his last encounter with Callum. Today, though, he knew he had a new challenge—improving his shooting. Dribbling had been about control and keeping the ball close, but shooting was different. The moment could change everything in a game, the difference between winning and losing.

Mason was already waiting, casually dribbling his ball as usual. As soon as Robin approached, Mason greeted him with a nod. "Ready for the next step?"

Robin smiled. "Yeah. What are we working on today?"

Mason held up the ball. "Shooting."

Robin's excitement grew, but Mason quickly added, "Don't get too excited. Most people think shooting's just about smashing the ball into the net. But to be a good shooter, you must balance power and precision."

Robin nodded, listening intently.

Mason set the ball down between them and began to explain. "Dribbling gets you through defenders, but shooting—that's what finishes the play. And it's not just about how hard you can kick. It's about knowing where to put the ball. You could kick it as hard as you want, but if it's straight at the goalkeeper, it won't matter."

He picked up the ball and demonstrated a quick instep shot, striking it with the laces of his boot. The ball flew straight and hard into the back of the net. "This is called the instep drive. You use your laces for power, but you've got to keep the shot on target. No wild kicks."

Robin watched closely, impressed by how smooth and controlled Mason's movement was.

"Your foot placement is key," Mason continued. "Plant your non-kicking foot next to the ball and strike with your laces when shooting. Follow through to keep the ball on target. It's all about power and accuracy together."

Robin stepped forward, ready to give it a try. He positioned the ball, planted his left foot next to it, and swung his right foot to strike with his laces. The ball flew off his foot, too high, and sailed over the crossbar.

"Too much power, not enough control," Mason said, but he wasn't harsh about it. "You've got the strength. Now, let's focus on aiming. Try again, but keep your shot lower this time."

Robin adjusted his stance and tried again, focusing on controlling the power in his strike. The ball stayed lower, but it was still off-target, missing wide of the goal. He sighed in frustration.

Mason walked over and clapped him on the shoulder. "Don't stress it. Shooting is one of the hardest skills to master because it's so easy to overthink. We'll get there."

They spent the next hour practising different types of shots. Mason demonstrated the finesse shot next, using the inside of his foot to curl the ball into the corner of the net. "This one's about placement, not power. If you're near the goal, you don't need to blast it. Just guide it past the keeper."

Robin gave it a try, and though his first attempts were weak, he began to feel the difference. He learned to aim for the corners, focusing on accuracy over force.

As the sun climbed higher in the sky, Mason set up cones in the four corners of the goal. "All right, let's test your precision. Whatever you choose, aim for the cones—top corners, bottom corners. The goal is to hit them cleanly."

Robin took a deep breath and lined up his first shot. He aimed for the bottom-left corner, struck the ball with his laces, and watched as it sailed across the target. He gritted his teeth but reset for another try. Slowly, his shots improved. Some hit the corners, others missed, but he got closer each time.

"Better," Mason said, watching closely. "You're starting to control the ball. But now, let's add some pressure."

Mason stepped into the goal and faced Robin. "In a real match, you never shoot at an empty net. You've got defenders and a keeper to beat. I'll be the keeper—try to get past me."

Robin felt a surge of nervous energy. He knew Mason wasn't going to make it easy. He lined up his shot and focused on the goal, trying to picture the ball flying into the corner.

Robin sent the ball toward the goal with a quick strike, but Mason moved quickly, diving to his right and blocking the shot. "Too predictable," Mason said, tossing the ball back. "You need to mix it up. Keep me guessing."

Robin tried again, this time faking a move to the left before shooting to the right. It was closer, but Mason still managed to block it.

As they continued the drill, Robin's frustration grew. He knew what to do, but getting the ball past Mason felt impossible. He was either overhitting or not putting enough power behind his shots. After several failed attempts, Robin stopped, panting.

"It's not just about power or accuracy," Mason said, walking over to Robin. "It's about staying calm. I can tell you're getting frustrated, which messes with your focus. When you're about to shoot, forget everything else. Please focus on the ball, the goal, and where you want to place it. Nothing else matters."

Robin nodded, wiping sweat from his brow. He stepped back to take his final shot of the session. This time, he closed his eyes briefly, visualising the ball flying into the top corner. He opened his eyes, lined up the shot, and struck the ball with his laces. It flew with power and accuracy, curving just enough to slip past Mason's outstretched hand and into the top corner of the net.

For a moment, Robin couldn't believe it. He'd done it— he'd hit the perfect shot.

Mason grinned, impressed. "Now that's what I'm talking about! You've got the power, and now you've got the precision. Keep practising like this, and you'll score in no time."

Robin couldn't stop smiling. He'd struggled, sure, but he'd broken through. He was learning to control the ball like never before, and it felt incredible.

As they wrapped up, Mason gave Robin one last piece of advice. "Shooting is as much about your mind as it is your foot. When you're under pressure, stay calm. Pick your spot and go for it."

Robin nodded, already looking forward to the next time he'd have the chance to test his shooting in a real game. The pieces were coming together, and he was starting to feel like a real player.

The Big Match

Determination

Determination is the fire within that drives you forward. Hold onto it, especially when the pressure is on.

The sun hung low over the park as Robin went to the field, soccer ball in hand. He could hear the familiar sounds of Callum and his group playing ahead of him, but this time, Robin didn't feel the same nervousness that used to twist his stomach into knots. He'd been practising for weeks—his dribbling was sharp, and his shooting had finally started to come together.

As he stepped onto the field, Callum spotted him. The usual smirk appeared on his face as Robin approached. "Look who's back. What do you want this time?" Callum sneered.

Robin glanced at the game and stepped forward. "I want to join in."

Callum raised an eyebrow, clearly not amused. "You? You think you can join because last time you were lucky?" He laughed, looking around at the other kids, who chuckled along. Robin's face remained calm. He had learned to control his frustration, to focus on what mattered. But Callum wasn't ready to make it easy.

"How about this," Callum said, stepping before Robin. "Let's make it interesting. One-on-one again! You shoot, I'll block. If you can score on me, then maybe, just maybe, I'll let you play." His challenge was clear, and Robin knew Callum wasn't expecting him to win. He was looking for another chance to embarrass Robin in front of the group.

The kids circled again, excited to watch the showdown. Callum prided himself on being the best player in the group, especially when it came to scoring and defending. But Robin wasn't the same player he had been before. He had worked too hard to back down now.

"Fine," Robin said, meeting Callum's gaze. "Let's do it."

Callum smirked, clearly underestimating Robin's determination. "All right, you've got five shots. Let's see if you can score."

Robin set the ball down at the edge of the box and took a deep breath. His first shot needed to be perfect. He lined up, planted his foot, and struck the ball with his laces, aiming for the bottom-left corner of the goal. Callum reacted quickly, diving to his right and blocking the shot easily.

The kids watching snickered, but Robin wasn't rattled. He'd learned to stay calm. He remembered Mason's advice: Pick your spot and go for it. Stay focused. He grabbed the ball, set it down again, and prepared for his next shot.

This time, he aimed for the top-right corner, curling the ball with the inside of his foot. It was close, but the ball clanged off the post just inches from the goal. Callum smirked, standing tall in the goal, but Robin didn't give him the satisfaction of seeing frustration. Instead, he reset.

As Robin lined up for his third attempt, Callum's confidence grew. "You sure you're ready for this, Robin?" he called out, but Robin didn't answer. He blocked out the noise, the taunts, everything. He could hear Mason's voice in his head: Forget everything else. Just focus on the ball, the goal, and your target.

Robin took a deep breath, fixed his eyes on the top-left corner, and struck the ball with his laces. It flew, curving perfectly; this time, it soared just beyond Callum's reach. The ball hit the back of the net, and everything seemed to go silent for a moment.

Robin had done it. He had scored.

The kids around the field stopped snickering. They stared at Robin, surprised. Callum, who had already been preparing a smug comment, was momentarily left speechless. He quickly shook off the surprise and barked, "Lucky shot. Let's see if you can do it again."

But Robin knew it wasn't luck. He had been working for this moment for weeks.

The next round began, and Robin was ready. This time, he used the finesse shot Mason had shown him, aiming to curl the ball around Callum. With a light touch and precise aim, the ball curled beautifully, tucking into the far corner of the net. Callum dove, but he was too late.

Another goal. Another silence from the group.

Now, the other kids were watching closely, not with mockery but with interest. They weren't laughing anymore—they were impressed. Robin had transformed right before their eyes, from the kid they could mock to someone they had to take seriously.

As the challenge continued, Robin scored again, this time with a volley that he had practised over and over. Callum, frustrated, could do nothing but mutter under his breath as the ball found the back of the net once again.

By the time the challenge ended, Robin had scored multiple times, proving that his shooting had dramatically improved. Callum, red-faced and irritated, kicked the ball back toward the middle of the field, but his grin disappeared. He couldn't pretend that Robin hadn't earned those goals.

One of the boys, Jake, who had watched the whole thing with wide eyes, approached Robin with a nod. "That was... pretty good, Robin. Didn't know you had it in you."

Robin smiled, the weight of weeks of practice lifting off his shoulders. "Thanks," he said, feeling a surge of pride.

Even Callum, though he was too proud to say much, gave a slight nod of acknowledgement. "Not bad, Robin," he muttered, still annoyed but impressed.

The other kids, who had once laughed at Robin's mistakes, now looked at him with newfound respect. Some of them even asked when he'd be back to play again.

Robin walked away from the field, feeling a rush of satisfaction. He had faced Callum again, but it was on his terms this time, and he had held his own. The hours of practice with Mason had paid off, and now Robin knew that he wasn't just improving—he was becoming the player he'd always wanted to be.

As he headed home, soccer ball under his arm, Robin smiled. This wasn't the end—it was only the beginning.

The Perfect Pass

Precision

Precision isn't just in the kick—it's in the intent.
Aim carefully, and let your passes be purposeful.

The park felt more familiar to Robin now. The nerves that had once held him down seemed to fade each time he came back. He had improved his dribbling, and his shooting had come together in ways he never imagined. Today, though, Mason was about to teach him a skill that could tie everything together—passing.

When Robin arrived, Mason was already waiting with his usual calm smile. "Ready to work on something new?"

Robin nodded eagerly. "What's the plan for today?"

Mason picked up the ball and twirled it in his hands. "Passing," he said. "Dribbling and shooting are great, but passing? That's the heart of the game. If you can't pass, you can't play as a team. And soccer is a team game, Robin."

Robin listened intently. He hadn't thought much about passing before, focusing more on controlling the ball. But Mason was right—the team couldn't function without good passing.

"Passing is about more than just kicking the ball to your teammate," Mason continued, placing the ball at his feet. "It's about making decisions, seeing the game unfold, and knowing where to pass it and when. The best players make their teammates better and do it with smart passing."

Robin was hooked. "So, how do I get better at that?"

Mason smiled. "Let's start with the basics."

He placed two cones about ten feet apart and instructed Robin to stand at one while he took the other. "We're going to work on short passes first. The most common and important kind. You want to use the inside of your foot to keep control, lock your ankle, and aim for accuracy, not power."

Mason demonstrated, making a clean, crisp pass to Robin. Robin controlled it quickly with the inside of his foot, mimicking Mason's technique as he passed the ball back. They continued this way, with Mason adjusting Robin's footwork and body position.

"Remember, Robin," Mason said between passes, "when you're passing, think about making it easy for your teammate to control. You want the ball to come to their feet cleanly. It's not about blasting the ball. Keep it simple and precise."

As Robin grew more comfortable with the short passes, Mason moved the cones further apart. "Now let's practice something trickier–the through ball. This pass splits defenders and sets up your teammate for a goal."

Mason explained the concept of a through ball while positioning himself further down the field. "You're not passing to where I am," Mason said, jogging in place. "You're passing to where I'm going to be. You have to anticipate the movement."

Robin took a breath and watched Mason as he began to jog lightly into space. Robin saw the gap between the imaginary defenders and aimed to pass the ball through it. His first attempt needed to be faster, arriving behind Mason. His second attempt had the proper power but was slightly off target.

"Timing's key here, Robin," Mason said encouragingly. "You've got to read the play and act just before the moment happens. It takes practice, but once you get it, you can unlock any defence."

After several more attempts, Robin began to improve. His passes became quicker and more precise, and Mason could run onto them in stride, creating what would have been perfect goal-scoring opportunities.

"Now you're getting it," Mason said with a nod of approval. "This kind of pass can change the game. One good through ball, and you've set up your teammate for a goal."

Robin's confidence was building, but Mason wasn't finished yet.

"Now, let's work on long passes," Mason said, placing cones farther away. "This is when you want to switch play or find a teammate on the other side of the field. It's all about power and accuracy."

Mason first struck the ball cleanly with his laces, sending it sailing smoothly through the air to land near one of the cones. "You've got to strike the ball low and hard with your laces, but don't lose control. It's like shooting—you want the ball to stay down, not fly over the goal."

Robin tried his first long pass, but it went too high, soaring well over the cones Mason had set as targets.

"Too much lift," Mason called out. "Focus on keeping the ball low. Power is good, but you need to control it."

Robin nodded, adjusting his stance. He took a deep breath and tried again, focusing on the power and the direction. This time, the ball stayed low and reached the target area.

"Much better," Mason said, giving him a thumbs up. "Now try hitting that cone again."

After several attempts, Robin's long passes began to find their mark. He was starting to feel the connection between power and precision, understanding how to strike the ball so it travelled far but stayed controlled.

Mason stepped back, watching as Robin practised. "You're learning fast. But remember, passing isn't just about technique—it's about vision. When you're in a game, you need to know where your teammates are, where the defenders are, and when to make the pass. It's about seeing the play before it happens."

Robin was beginning to understand. Passing wasn't just about moving the ball and making the right decisions at the right time.

After a few more drills, Robin felt his confidence rising. He improved at reading the field, finding the right moment to pass, and making accurate, controlled passes. But there was still one thing he needed to master—timing.

Mason set up one final drill. He jogged toward the goal, and Robin had to time his through ball perfectly. Robin watched closely, feeling the rhythm of the game. As Mason approached the imaginary defenders, Robin struck the ball, sending it ideally through the gap and into Mason's path. Mason controlled the ball quickly and shot it into the goal.

"That's it, Robin!" Mason called, running back. "Perfect timing, perfect pass. Keep that up, and you'll set goals left and right."

Robin beamed. He had struggled at first, but now he saw the game differently. Passing wasn't just a skill—it was the glue that held everything together.

As they wrapped up, Mason patted Robin on the back. "You've come a long way, but there's always more to learn. Just remember, the best players are the ones who make their teammates better. And the best way to do that is through great passing."

Robin nodded, feeling a new sense of accomplishment. He was learning that soccer wasn't just about individual brilliance—it was about teamwork, vision, and making the right moves at the right time.

Passing with Purpose

Intention

When you play with purpose, every pass has meaning.
Make each move count.

The sun was dipping low in the sky as Robin went to the park. His heart felt steady, more sure of itself than in weeks. He had spent countless hours practising dribbling, shooting, and now passing. Today, he was ready to put it all together.

As he approached the field, he saw the familiar sight of Callum, Jake, and the rest of the boys playing their usual game. Robin felt a small surge of excitement. This time, he wasn't just hoping to keep up—he was ready to make an impact.

Jake, a tall and athletic boy with short, spiked black hair and intense dark brown eyes, waved him over. Jake played mostly in midfield, always calm under pressure, and had a natural ability to read the game. He wasn't flashy like Callum, but his intelligence and vision made him one of the most important players on the field. He was known for his sharp decision-making and his ability to find open spaces and create plays for his teammates.

"Robin! Join our side!" Jake called out. Callum glanced at Robin but didn't argue. His expression wasn't welcoming but lacked the dismissive mockery from weeks ago.

Robin jogged onto the field, sliding into his position. The game started quickly, the ball moving back and forth, but Robin knew he wouldn't force anything this time. He'd learned from Mason that passing wasn't about rushing—it was about control, vision, and timing. His job was to keep the game moving and find the right moments.

The first few passes were simple—short, sharp passes to teammates, keeping possession and maintaining the game's rhythm. Robin focused on making each pass clean, aiming for his teammates' feet to make their jobs easier. He could feel the game flowing, his mind calm as he anticipated the next move.

Jake, playing his usual role in midfield, was watching Robin closely. Robin had improved in passing, and Jake noticed. As the ball came to Robin again, Jake gave him a quick nod, signalling for him to take control. "Keep your head up, Robin, and find the space. You've got this," Jake encouraged. It was a subtle gesture, but Robin felt the confidence growing inside him.

But Callum's team wasn't about to make it easy. The pressure began to build as they closed in on Robin every time he touched the ball, trying to force him into a mistake. Robin could feel the heat of their presence, but instead of panicking, he stayed focused.

Mason's words echoed in his mind: *Keep your vision. Know where your teammates are. Make the smart pass.*

Then came the moment he had been waiting for. Jake was running toward the goal, and Robin saw it before anyone else did. The defenders hadn't caught on yet, but there was a gap—just big enough for Robin to slip the ball through. Without hesitation, he struck the ball precisely, between the defenders, right into Jake's path.

Jake didn't miss a beat. With his typical calm under pressure, he sprinted onto the ball and fired it into the back of the net with the precision of a seasoned midfielder. Jake wasn't just scoring the goal—he had made the perfect run, anticipating Robin's pass. This was the kind of play that Jake excelled at, finding the right spaces and making smart decisions.

The goal was met with cheers, and Robin felt a surge of pride. He didn't need to score the goal—he had created it.

"Great pass, Robin!" Jake called out, jogging back to high-five him. The other boys nodded in approval, even those on the opposing team. Robin felt a rush of satisfaction. He had made an impact.

But Callum wasn't happy. Robin could see the frustration building as the game wore on. Every time Robin touched the ball, Callum's team tried to shut him down, but Robin wasn't fazed. He kept the ball moving, making quick passes to his teammates, switching the play when needed, and finding the open spaces.

Jake stayed close, acting as a calming influence, always ready to provide support when needed. "You're reading the game well, Robin," Jake said after another successful pass. "Keep it up. You've got an eye for this." Hearing this from Jake, one of the team's smartest players, was all the encouragement Robin needed.

As the game continued, Robin noticed something else—his teammates were looking to him to control the game's flow. They trusted his decisions, passing the ball to him when they needed direction. It was a new feeling for Robin, being a key player, not just another body on the field.

With the score tied and the game nearing its end, Robin found himself in possession once more. He scanned the field, looking for an opening. One of his teammates ran toward the far post, slipping past the defenders. Robin knew this was his moment.

He took a deep breath, lined up the long pass, and struck the ball with his laces. It soared through the air, low and fast, curving toward the far side of the field. The ball landed perfectly at his teammate's feet just as he reached the edge of the box. Without hesitation, his teammate slotted the ball into the net.

Robin's team erupted in cheers as the final whistle blew. They had won.

As the boys gathered around, Robin felt the weight of their eyes on him. They no longer looked at him as the kid who struggled to keep up. They saw him as someone who could control the game and make things happen.

Jake clapped him on the back. "That was amazing, Robin. You've got an eye for this," he said with a smile.

Even Callum, though annoyed by the loss, gave a reluctant nod. "You've gotten a lot better," he muttered. It wasn't much, but it felt like real recognition from Callum.

Robin smiled, feeling the satisfaction of all his hard work paying off. He didn't need Callum's approval anymore. He knew he had earned his place on the field.

As he walked off the field, soccer ball tucked under his arm, Robin felt lighter than he had in weeks. He wasn't just a kid trying to keep up with the others anymore—he was a player, an essential part of the team. And for the first time, he knew he would only get better.

The Final Tackle

Persistence
Persistence is pushing forward when others would stop. Don't give up until the game is truly over.

Robin arrived at the park earlier than usual. He had been on a roll lately—his passing had improved dramatically, and he was starting to feel like a key player on the field. But today, Mason had promised to teach him something new, and Robin was eager to learn. As soon as he saw Mason waiting by the edge of the field, he jogged over, ready to start.

Mason gave Robin a nod of approval. "You've been doing great, Robin. Your dribbling, shooting, and passing are all coming together. But there's one more part of your game that needs work."

Robin tilted his head, curious. "What's that?"

"Defending," Mason replied. "Everyone loves to score goals, but great teams are built on a solid defence. A good defender can change the entire game."

Robin hadn't thought much about defending before. He was always focused on attacking, trying to score or create chances for his teammates. But Mason's words made sense. It didn't matter how many goals a team could score without a strong defence.

"Defending isn't just about stopping the ball," Mason continued. "It's about reading the game, knowing where to position yourself, and being patient. You can't rush in blindly—you've got to wait for the right moment to make your move."

Robin nodded, already starting to understand the importance of this new skill. "So, how do I get better at it?"

Mason smiled. "Let's start with the basics."

He positioned Robin about ten feet away from him, with a soccer ball at Mason's feet. "One of the most important things you'll learn as a defender is jockeying. It's how you control the space between you and the attacker, keeping pressure on them without diving in too soon."

Mason dribbled the ball slowly toward Robin, and Robin instinctively rushed forward, trying to take the ball. But Mason sidestepped quickly, moving past him with minimal effort.

"Too fast," Mason said, shaking his head. "You don't want to commit too early. Stay on your feet, keep me before you, and wait for the right moment."

Robin tried again, staying back and carefully watching Mason's movements. As Mason advanced, Robin adjusted his position, staying in front of him and blocking his path. When Mason tries to make a move, Robin can stick with him, forcing him wide and out of danger.

"Better," Mason said with a nod. "Remember, you're not trying to win the ball right away. Your job is to guide the attacker into a position where they can't hurt you."

Next, Mason moved on to tackle. "When it comes to tackling, timing is everything. You'll either miss or foul the attacker if you rush in too soon. You've got to wait when they lose control of the ball, then step in and take it cleanly."

Mason dribbled toward Robin again, this time more aggressively. Robin waited, watching for his chance. As Mason made a slight mistake, letting the ball drift too far ahead, Robin pounced. He stepped in quickly, using his foot to knock the ball away and regain possession.

"Perfect," Mason said with a smile. "That's how you do it—wait for the right moment, then act."

They spent the next half-hour practising different tackling techniques, with Robin learning to anticipate Mason's movements and time his tackles with precision. Robin felt a surge of satisfaction each time he made a clean tackle. He was beginning to see the game from a different perspective—not just as an attacker, but as someone who could stop attacks and control the game's flow.

Finally, Mason set up the last drill: interceptions. "A good defender doesn't just chase the ball," Mason explained. "They read the play, position themselves where the ball will be, and cut off passes before they reach the attacker."

Mason lined up a series of passes, and Robin had to read the play and step in to intercept. At first, it was tough—Robin was still thinking like an attacker, trying to chase the ball instead of predicting where it was going. But as he practised more, he began to improve, learning to watch Mason's body language and anticipate the direction of the pass.

After several tries, Robin finally got it. He perfectly intercepted one of Mason's passes, stepping in front of the imaginary attacker and cutting off the ball before reaching them.

"Great job, Robin," Mason said, clapping him on the back. "You're getting it. Defending isn't just about being physical—it's about being smart, reading the game, and putting yourself in the right place at the right time."

Robin nodded, feeling a new sense of accomplishment. He had always considered defending simple—just stopping the other team from scoring. But now, he understood how much strategy and patience were involved.

As they wrapped up the session, Mason gave Robin one final piece of advice. "Remember, defending is as important as scoring goals. A great defender can change the outcome of a game. If you can master both sides of the ball—attacking and defending—you'll be unstoppable."

Robin smiled, feeling a new sense of confidence. He was starting to see the game in a new light, and he couldn't wait to put his defence skills to the test in the next match.

Defending the Dream

Resilience
Dreams are worth defending—stand firm and protect them, even when the odds are against you.

Robin could feel the familiar buzz of excitement as he walked to the park. But this time, there was something different about it. He wasn't just another player hoping to fit in or trying to prove himself as a goal-scorer. He was coming to the field with a new purpose—to defend, to stop attacks, and to control the game from the back.

The boys were already in the middle of a game when he arrived. Liam, a tall and muscular defender with short-cropped dark hair and piercing green eyes, gave him a nod as Robin joined the field. Liam had a strong, silent presence, and everyone on the team knew that with him in defence, they had a rock they could rely on. "You're with us today," Liam said, his deep voice calm but commanding.

Robin nodded, quickly stepping into position. He knew today was going to be different. Today, he would show them that he wasn't just about scoring goals or making passes. Today, he was ready to be the last line of defence, just like Liam.

The game started fast. The ball moved back and forth, with both teams fighting for control. Robin stayed focused, keeping his eyes on Callum, who, as usual, was trying to dominate the field with his dribbling and attacking play. Robin knew that, eventually, Callum would come at him.

And he did.

Callum picked up the ball near midfield and drove toward Robin's team. His footwork was sharp, and he quickly skipped past a couple of Robin's teammates. Now, it was just Callum, the ball, and Robin.

This was the moment Robin had been waiting for. He remembered Mason's words: *Don't dive in too early. Stay patient. Guide him away from the goal.*

Callum came straight at him, his confidence clear. Robin planted his feet and began jockeying, staying low and keeping his body between Callum and the goal. He didn't rush in; he didn't panic. He just stayed with Callum, forcing him to move wide, away from the danger zone.

Liam, standing behind Robin, watched silently. Robin could feel Liam's presence, like a wall of strength, backing him up if needed. Liam never rushed in either—he knew when to wait and when to act, always in the right spot to cover his teammates.

Robin could see the frustration starting to grow on Callum's face. He wasn't getting through quickly like he had before. Robin cut off his angles, giving him no clear path to shoot or pass.

"Come on, Robin!" Callum taunted, trying to bait him into making a mistake. But Robin wasn't falling for it. He kept his focus, blocking Callum's options.

Then it happened—just a slight slip from Callum. The ball drifted too far from his feet, and Robin saw his chance. Instantly, he stepped in with a clean tackle, winning the ball and knocking it upfield.

Liam gave a rare nod of approval, his green eyes sharp. "Solid tackle," he said quietly. "You've got a good sense for defending." His voice was low, but Robin could feel the weight of the compliment. Liam didn't speak often, but when he did, it meant something.

Callum was left standing in frustration as the ball moved away from him. Robin felt a surge of pride. He had done it. He had stopped Callum in his tracks.

The game continued, and Robin was in the thick of it, making critical defensive plays. He cut off passes, intercepting the ball before reaching the attackers. He stayed calm under pressure, positioning himself perfectly to block Callum and the other attackers from making dangerous moves.

Liam was always nearby, stepping in when needed. His physical strength made him an intimidating force, but it was his timing and positioning that made him a great defender. He didn't chase after the ball—he waited for the perfect moment to strike, showing Robin the importance of patience.

Then, in the game's final minutes, Callum's team won a corner kick. It was a crucial moment—the score was tied, and a goal could decide the game. Robin knew this was it. This was the time to prove himself as a complete player.

As the ball sailed in from the corner, Robin watched it closely, reading its flight. Callum was in the box, ready to move, but Robin was ready. He timed his jump perfectly, rising above the others and meeting the ball with a firm header, clearing it far from danger.

Liam stepped in to shield the ball from Callum as it was cleared, using his body to protect it and help his team transition to attack. "Good clearance, Robin," he said as the play moved forward. His approval was understated but powerful.

The ball flew out of the box, and within seconds, Robin's team was back on the attack. They scored on the counter, sealing the win. The game was over.

As the final whistle blew, Robin's teammates congratulated him. Liam walked over, his expression still calm but a slight smile on his face. "You held the line well today," Liam said, clapping Robin on the back. "You're getting stronger in defence."

Even Callum, though visibly frustrated by being shut down, gave a grudging nod of acknowledgement. "You did well today," he muttered.

Robin didn't need more than that. He had earned their respect, not just as an attacker or passer, but as a defender—a complete player.

Robin felt deeply satisfied as he walked off the field, soccer ball in hand. He had mastered a new skill that made all the difference. He wasn't just a kid trying to keep up anymore. He was a key player who could make a real impact on both sides of the game.

Robin smiled to himself. He knew there were more challenges ahead and more skills to learn, but today, he had proven something important. He had become the defender his team needed.

Mastering the Midfield

Control

Control the field, control the game. Keep a steady mind, and the rest will follow.

Robin arrived at the park, eager for his next session with Mason. He had learned to dribble, shoot, pass, and defend, but today, Mason had promised to teach him something different—something that didn't rely as much on physical skill but more on the mental side of the game.

When he reached the field, Mason greeted him with a knowing smile. "You've improved a lot, Robin. But there's one skill that ties everything together—positioning."

Robin raised an eyebrow. "Positioning?"

Mason nodded. "You can be the best player technically, but if you're not in the right place at the right time, it won't matter. Positioning is about reading the game, knowing where to be and when to move. It's what makes great players stand out."

Robin thought about the games he'd played recently. There were moments when he felt lost, unsure of where to go, and other times when the ball seemed to come straight to him as if by luck. But now he realised—it wasn't luck. It was positioning.

"Positioning isn't just for when you have the ball," Mason continued. "It's about knowing where the space is, where the defenders are, and where your teammates need you to be. And it's just as important on defence. You often don't even need to make a tackle—just being in the right place can stop an attack."

Robin nodded, excited to learn more. "So, how do I get better at it?"

Mason set up a grid on the field with cones and had Robin stand at the centre. "First, you need to be aware of everything around you—the ball, your teammates, the defenders, and the open space. Let's work on your space awareness."

They started with a simple drill where Mason moved the ball around, and Robin had to adjust his position, always staying in the best spot to either receive a pass or block a potential attack. At first, Robin found it challenging to keep track of everything—he was used to focusing on just the ball. But as the drill continued, he began to see the bigger picture, understanding that positioning wasn't just about the ball and the entire field.

"Good," Mason said as Robin moved to receive a pass. "Now, let's step it up."

Mason started running a few simulated plays, forcing Robin to read the game and get into the proper position based on how the play unfolded. He had to predict where the ball would go and be there, ready to pass, shoot, or defend. It was tough at first—Robin often arrived too late, missing the chance to make an impact.

"Positioning is about anticipation," Mason explained. "Don't wait for the ball to come to you—see where it will be and get there first. The best players are the ones who know what's going to happen before it happens."

After several repetitions, Robin started to catch on. He began moving into space before the ball got there, making himself available for passes and cutting off potential attacks before they could develop. It was like seeing the game in a whole new way.

Next, Mason moved on to transition drills. "In a real game, you'll constantly switch between attack and defence. Your positioning needs to adjust quickly. You've got to be ready to support the attack when your team wins the ball and drop back to defend when you lose it."

They practised scenarios where Robin's team lost possession, forcing him to drop back quickly and get into a defensive position. Then, when his team regained the ball, he had to shift into an attacking role, getting into space to help build the play. It was challenging, but Robin could feel himself improving with each repetition.

After a while, Mason stopped the drill and smiled. "You're getting it, Robin. Positioning is more than just standing in the right spot—it's about reading the game, thinking ahead, and always being ready for what comes next."

Finally, they moved on to a transition play. Mason played as an opposing attacker, and Robin had to read the game and adjust his positioning based on whether his team was attacking or defending. As Mason moved toward a goal, Robin positioned himself perfectly to block the attack, forcing Mason wide. Then, when Robin's team regained possession, he quickly transitioned, moving into space to receive a pass and set up the next play.

It all came together in a moment of perfect timing. Robin intercepted Mason's pass, made a quick run forward, and delivered a pass to a teammate in space, creating a goal-scoring opportunity. The success filled Robin with confidence. Positioning wasn't just about being fast or strong—it was about seeing the game, thinking ahead, and being where he needed to be.

As they wrapped up the session, Mason clapped Robin on the back. "You've come a long way, Robin. Positioning is what separates good players from great ones. You're starting to see the game differently now. Keep working on it; you'll always be one step ahead."

Robin smiled, feeling a deep sense of accomplishment. He was learning more than just how to play soccer—he was learning how to think the game. And with Mason's guidance, he was becoming the complete player he had always wanted to be.

Being in the Right Time at the Right Place

Awareness
Awareness opens doors others don't see. Know where you stand and how to make the most of it.

The air felt crisp as Robin stepped onto the park field, a soccer ball tucked under his arm. His heart beat steadily—not with nerves, but with quiet confidence. He had been practising hard, and he was ready to show it today. Today wasn't about flashy dribbling or hard tackles. It was about positioning, about being in the right place at the right time.

As Robin joined the usual group of boys, they quickly called him to join the game. "Robin, you're with us!" Jake shouted, as usual, waving him over to their side. Robin smiled, slipping into his position.

Standing nearby was Ethan, a shorter, lean boy with messy light brown hair and sharp hazel eyes. Ethan wasn't loud or flashy, but he was quick and always seemed to be in the right place at the right time. Robin had seen him play before–Ethan's positioning was impeccable, and he often slipped into spaces unnoticed by the opposition. "You ready?" Ethan asked quietly, giving Robin a small nod. Robin nodded back, already feeling a sense of connection with the way Ethan moved around the field.

When the game started, Robin knew he had to focus on more than just where the ball was. He kept his eyes moving, tracking both his teammates and the opposition. Every step was calculated, every movement deliberate. He wasn't just running for the sake of it–he was positioning himself for the next play.

Callum, as usual, tried to dominate the game, darting up the field with his usual flair. But Robin had already positioned himself defensively, blocking Callum's route. He wasn't chasing Callum or the ball but cut off Callum's angles, forcing him wide and away from danger. Callum's frustration was visible as Robin calmly took up space, making it impossible for him to dribble toward the goal.

Callum eventually passed the ball, unable to find a way through. Robin smiled to himself, realising how effective positioning could be. He hadn't touched the ball but stopped Callum's attack before it started.

"Nice job," Ethan said, stepping closer to Robin during a break in play. "Positioning is everything. You didn't even need to tackle him." Ethan's eyes flicked back to the game, constantly reading the movement of players. "Stay aware of where the space opens up. That's where you'll make the difference."

As the game flowed, Robin became increasingly involved—not just in defence, but in helping his team control the play. He didn't always need the ball to make an impact. Instead, he positioned himself where he could be most helpful. Whether to receive a pass, block an opponent, or support a teammate, Robin was ready.

Midway through the game, Callum's team launched a quick counter-attack. Robin immediately dropped back, scanning the field. Callum was leading the charge, pushing the ball upfield with speed. But Robin didn't panic. He moved into the correct position, cutting Callum's path to goal.

As Callum dribbled closer, Robin stayed patient. He didn't dive in or overcommit. He held his ground, guiding Callum away from the goal. Frustrated, Callum tried to move past him quickly, but Robin had anticipated it. He stepped in and intercepted the ball cleanly, quickly sending it upfield to his teammate Jake.

Ethan jogged over, giving Robin a quiet nod. "You're reading the game well. Keep positioning like that, and you'll always have the advantage." Robin appreciated Ethan's calm encouragement—it wasn't loud praise, but it meant a lot coming from someone who seemed to instinctively understand positioning.

The game continued, and Robin's positioning started to shine. His teammates began to rely on him more, trusting that he would be in the right place at the right time. Whether moving into space to receive a pass or blocking the opposition's attack, Robin was always one step ahead.

In the final minutes of the game, the score was tied. Robin's team had one last chance to win. As they moved upfield, Robin saw an opportunity developing. He moved into space near the edge of the box, watching as his teammates struggled to break through the defence. Suddenly, a gap opened up.

Without hesitating, Robin darted into the open space. His teammate saw the move and passed the ball. Robin received it perfectly, his positioning allowing him to take control of the play. With one quick touch, he laid the ball off to another teammate, who fired it into the back of the net.

The whistle blew. Robin's team had won.

Ethan walked over, his hazel eyes scanning the field as if still analysing the game. "That last move—you saw the space before anyone else did. Well done, Robin. You've got an eye for this."

Robin's teammates crowded around him as they celebrated, clapping him on the back. Jake grinned. "You were everywhere today, Robin. Always in the right spot. That pass at the end was perfect."

Even Callum, though visibly frustrated, couldn't help but acknowledge Robin's performance. "You've gotten good, Robin," he muttered, giving him a begrudging nod.

Robin smiled, feeling a deep sense of satisfaction. Today, he hadn't been about scoring goals or making flashy moves. It had been about positioning—reading the game, anticipating what would happen next, and being in the right place to make a difference. And he had done precisely that.

As he walked off the field, soccer ball under his arm, Robin felt more confident than ever. He knew that his understanding of the game had grown. He wasn't just reacting anymore—he was shaping the game, controlling the flow, and ensuring his team was always one step ahead.

Positioning had made him a more competent, complete player, and he couldn't wait to keep building on that.

Speed and Agility

Quickness
Quickness isn't just in your feet; it's in your mind.
Be ready to adapt at any moment.

Robin jogged onto the park field, the cool morning air filling his lungs. He had mastered positioning, passing, and defending, but today, Mason would train him on something he knew would push him to the next level—speed and agility. The anticipation of the session made his pulse quicken. Speed wasn't just about running fast; Robin had started to understand that. Today, he was about to dig into what made players quick and hard to catch.

Mason stood by the edge of the field, already setting up cones in zigzag patterns. As Robin approached, Mason gave him a nod. "You're getting better each week, Robin. But speed and agility—that's what will make you dangerous."

Robin grinned, feeling a mix of excitement and determination. "I'm ready."

"Good. But remember, this isn't just about how fast you can run in a straight line," Mason said. "Speed in soccer is about those first few steps, how quickly you can react, how fast you can turn, and whether you can keep control. We're going to push those skills today."

Robin's grin faded as he realised how much was going into this training session. Speed wasn't just physical—it was mental, too. He nodded, trying to soak in Mason's words.

Mason started by setting up a series of cones about 10 yards apart. "We'll start with acceleration," Mason said. "The game moves fast, but you don't always need to sprint the field's length. What matters is how quickly you can reach top speed in just a few steps."

Robin positioned himself at the starting line, focusing on his stance. Mason crouched beside him, adjusting Robin's feet. "Lean slightly forward. Use your arms—they're as important as your legs. When you hear 'Go,' I want you to explode off the ground like you're launching forward. Drive with your legs and pump your arms hard."

Robin tightened his fists, took a deep breath, and waited. "Go!" Mason called.

Robin surged forward, but as he ran, he realised he wasn't moving as smoothly as he'd hoped. His legs felt heavy, and he was panting by the time he reached the last cone. Mason walked over, a thoughtful expression on his face.

"Not bad, but you're relying too much on your legs and not enough on your whole body. Speed comes from the first step. Your upper body should be working as hard as your legs."

Mason demonstrated, his body perfectly aligned as he launched from a standing start, covering ground quickly with smooth, powerful strides. Robin watched, impressed at how effortless it seemed.

"Your turn," Mason said, stepping aside.

Robin lined up again, mentally preparing to focus on his whole body—his arms, legs, and posture. "Go!" Mason called out, and this time, Robin shot forward, his arms pumping in rhythm with his legs. The difference was immediate. He felt lighter, faster, and more powerful. The ground seemed to fly beneath him.

"Better!" Mason called as Robin finished the sprint. "Now that's the explosion you need in a game."

They repeated the drill several times, and Robin felt more in control each time, his acceleration becoming sharper, faster. But he knew this was only one part of the training. After a few sprints, Mason moved to the next part of the session—agility.

"Speed is great, but in soccer, it's all about how quickly you can change direction," Mason said, motioning toward the zigzag pattern of cones he had set up earlier. "You can be fast in a straight line, but if you can't turn quickly or react to what's happening around you, that speed won't help. This drill will test how fast and sharp you can turn while staying in control."

Robin nodded, feeling a new kind of challenge ahead of him. He stepped up to the first cone, waiting for Mason's instructions.

"You want to stay low through this," Mason said, demonstrating how to drop his centre of gravity. "When you change direction, don't stand tall—bend your knees, stay low, and use the outside of your foot to push off. Your turns should be sharp, not wide."

Robin took a deep breath and started through the cones. The first few turns were awkward—he was turning too wide and losing momentum. But Mason stopped him and adjusted his stance.

"Stay lower. Keep your feet light, almost like you're bouncing between steps. It's not just about moving your feet quickly. You need to pivot sharply and use the ground to help you turn."

Robin tried again, this time staying low and focusing on each turn. He weaved between the cones, keeping his feet light, his movements sharper. By the third run, he moved faster, making quicker turns without losing his balance. The burn in his legs was intense, but Robin didn't mind. He could feel himself getting faster, his body learning to move more efficiently.

Mason clapped as Robin completed the drill again. "That's the speed we're looking for! Quick feet, sharp turns. You're starting to see how agility can make you unpredictable on the field."

But the session wasn't over yet. Now, it was time to combine everything. Mason set up a final drill—dribbling at speed. "Now, let's add the ball," Mason said, rolling a soccer ball toward Robin. "It's one thing to move fast, but can you do it while controlling the ball?"

Robin stared at the ball, knowing this would be the hardest part. He was used to dribbling, but doing it at top speed while making quick turns? That was a different challenge. He positioned himself at the start and began weaving through the cones, dribbling the ball. His first attempt was rough–his touches were too heavy, and he lost control halfway through.

"Smaller touches," Mason called. "The faster you move, the lighter your touch needs to be. Keep the ball close to your feet, especially when you turn."

Robin tried again, focusing on controlling the ball while maintaining his speed. His second run was better. He stayed lower, moved faster, and kept the ball tighter to his feet. As he finished the drill, he felt the familiar surge of satisfaction from improvement.

"That's it!" Mason cheered. "Speed, control, and balance. Put it all together, and you'll be untouchable."

By the end of the session, Robin was exhausted but proud. His legs burned, but it was a good kind of burn that told him he was getting faster, sharper. Mason smiled at him as they wrapped up. "You're on your way, Robin. Speed and agility aren't just about running fast–they're about moving smart and staying in control. Keep working on it, and you'll see the difference in the next game."

Robin grinned, wiping sweat from his forehead. He couldn't wait to put his new skills to the test. He was faster, more agile, and more in control than ever. And the next time he faced Callum and the others, he knew he'd be ready.

Quick Turns, Sharp Reactions

Flexibility
The game changes fast—stay flexible and let each sharp turn reveal new possibilities.

Robin arrived at the park feeling different. His legs were more robust, his body lighter, and his mind sharper. Mason's training had pushed him, and today was the day to see if it had all paid off. As he stepped onto the field, he could feel the anticipation buzzing.

The usual group of boys was already deep into their game when Jake spotted Robin. "Robin, you're with us!" Jake called out, waving him over.

Robin jogged onto the field, feeling a new level of confidence. This wasn't the same nervous energy he used to feel. Today, he was ready to prove that his speed and agility weren't just practice—they were real. He scanned the field, looking for his moment.

Standing nearby was Dylan, an average-height boy with long legs that gave him an elegant stride. His short blond hair and sharp blue eyes added to his intense presence on the field. As a defensive back, Dylan was known for his calm composure and ability to react quickly under pressure, using his long legs to cover a lot of ground.

The game kicked off quickly, and for the first few minutes, Robin focused on positioning himself and watching how the play unfolded. He could see the gaps opening and closing, the spaces where he could move. And then, his moment came.

The ball was passed to him on the wing, and instead of looking for a quick pass, Robin decided to take a chance. He remembered Mason's words: "Speed isn't just about running fast. It's about exploding forward, moving with purpose."

Robin took off. His first step was decisive, and he accelerated down the sideline, quickly gaining speed. Two defenders rushed toward him, but Robin didn't hesitate. He cut between them, using his quick feet to change direction just before they could reach him. His speed surprised them, and he was already gone by the time they reacted.

"Go, Robin!" Jake shouted from the midfield, watching in awe as Robin burst past the defenders. Robin grinned, the wind whipping past him as he surged forward. His speed felt effortless.

Dylan, standing near the backline, watched carefully. He admired Robin's speed but stayed focused on how

Robin would handle the next challenge, his blue eyes tracking every movement.

But then, standing in his way was Callum. Robin had been waiting for this moment—Callum, always the one to shut him down in the past. But today, Robin was faster and wiser. He approached Callum at full speed, but instead of trying to go straight through, he remembered the agility drills with Mason. He lowered his centre of gravity, kept his feet light, and as Callum lunged to block him, Robin cut sharply to the left.

Callum stumbled, caught off guard by the sudden change of direction. Robin didn't slow down. With a burst of speed, he accelerated past Callum, leaving him in the dust. The field opened up in front of him.

Robin could hear his teammates shouting as he sprinted toward the goal, but he stayed focused. His body moved effortlessly, each step measured and precise. The goalkeeper rushed out ahead of him, trying to close the distance.

Robin knew he had to stay calm. "Balance," Mason had told him. "Stay balanced, keep control, even when moving fast."

The goalkeeper dived to his left, but Robin was already one step ahead. He cut right, keeping his balance, and slotted the ball into the back of the net—the game-winning goal.

The field erupted with cheers from his teammates. Jake ran over, laughing and clapping Robin on the back. "That was incredible! You just flew past them!"

Even Callum, though frustrated, walked over. His eyes narrowed, but his voice showed a hint of respect. "You're faster than before," he muttered, giving Robin a slight nod.

Robin smiled, knowing what that acknowledgement meant. Callum was tough to impress, but Robin had done it. His speed and agility had made the difference.

Dylan approached Robin as they walked off the field. "You've got speed, Robin. Real speed," he said, his blue eyes still focused and analysing. "But remember, it's not just about reaction. Anticipate. You did well today, but think ahead—before the defenders can even close in. That's how you'll always stay one step ahead."

Robin nodded, appreciating the feedback. Dylan wasn't one to offer praise easily, but his advice carried weight. Robin could feel his game evolving—not just physically but mentally, too.

As the game wound down, Robin couldn't stop smiling. He felt the satisfaction of seeing his hard work pay off in a real game. Every sprint, every turn, every sharp cut had brought him closer to this moment. He wasn't just keeping up with the others anymore—he was outpacing them.

Walking off the field, Robin felt lighter than ever. His speed and agility had turned him into a player who could change the game with quickness and control. He had outmanoeuvred Callum, outrun the defenders, and finished with confidence.

Robin knew that this was just the beginning. His journey wasn't over, but today was a significant step forward. He was faster, more agile, and more in control of his game than ever.

More Than Just Soccer

Connection
Friendship goes beyond the field; it's about sharing who we are beyond the game. Together, we're not just teammates—we're friends, each bringing something unique that makes our bond stronger.

As the boys gathered around after the game, they started chatting about more than just soccer. Liam, Jake, Dylan, and Robin were standing together, sharing a moment of relaxation after the intensity of the match.

Jake grinned, nudging Robin. "So, what do you do when you're not out here playing soccer? We can't all be training like you every day," he joked.

Robin smiled. "I like to read, actually. I know it sounds a bit boring, but I've been into adventure stories lately. They kind of help me get away from all the noise."

Jake's eyes lit up. "No way! I'm into those, too. I've been reading this series about a group of kids who explore different places and solve mysteries. We should trade books sometime."

Robin chuckled. "Deal. I didn't know you were into reading. You always seemed more about the action."

Liam, standing beside them, chimed in. "You know, I'm into mountain biking. I like the freedom of just riding through trails and being out in nature. It's kind of like soccer in a way—you have to focus, react quickly, and there's this rush when you hit a tricky part of the trail."

Robin's eyes widened. "I've always wanted to try mountain biking! I didn't know you were into that, Liam. We should go riding sometime."

Liam smiled, giving Robin a nod. "Absolutely. We'll get you on the trails, and you'll love it. It's a good break from soccer, too."

Dylan leaned against the goalpost, listening quietly before adding, "I'm into puzzles. Not just the ones you put together, but logic puzzles and brain teasers. It's like solving a problem step by step. Kind of like how we play defence—strategising, staying ahead of the opponent."

Robin nodded. "That sounds interesting. I've done a few puzzles myself. Maybe you could show me some of your favourites."

Dylan smiled slightly. "Sure. It's a good way to keep the mind sharp—on and off the field."

Jake laughed, glancing at the group. "Look at us. Who knew we all had these different hobbies? But that's cool—it kind of shows we're not just a bunch of soccer players.

We've got more going on, and I think that makes us better friends too."

Liam grinned. "Yeah, we've got different things we're into, but I think that's what makes this group work. Robin, you're fitting right in—not just on the field, but with us. You're one of us now, no question."

Robin looked around at his friends, feeling a deep sense of belonging. "I'm glad. I couldn't ask for better teammates—or friends."

Mastering the Touch

Finesse
Finesse is the art of the delicate touch; it's in the moments when strength alone isn't enough.

Robin arrived at the park, eager for another session with Mason. He had worked on speed and agility, and now Mason had something new for him—ball control. It was a skill Robin knew he needed, especially after noticing how easily he could lose the ball when pressured by defenders. Today, he would learn how to keep the ball close, no matter what.

Mason greeted him with a nod. "You've gotten faster, Robin. But speed is nothing if you can't control the ball. Ball control is what makes a great player. It's the foundation of everything—dribbling, passing, shooting. If you can't control the ball, you won't be able to use any of your other skills effectively."

Robin listened carefully as Mason explained the importance of ball control. "It's all about touch. The ball must stay close to you whether you're receiving a pass or dribbling through defenders. The better your control, the more time you'll have to make decisions—and the less chance defenders have to steal it."

Robin nodded, understanding. He had seen the top players in action—how the ball seemed glued to their feet, how they moved so smoothly even under pressure. He wanted that.

"Let's start with the first touch," Mason said, setting up the first drill. "This is the most important part of ball control. If your first touch is bad, you'll spend more time chasing the ball than making plays."

Mason stood at one end of the field while Robin stood at the other. "I'm going to send you passes from different distances and angles," Mason explained. "Your job is to trap the ball close to your feet. Don't let it bounce away from you."

Mason sent the first pass, and Robin stopped it with his foot, but the ball bounced slightly away. "Too much force," Mason called out. "Cushion the ball with your foot. Let it settle under you."

Robin tried again, this time focusing on softening his touch. The next pass came, and Robin trapped it with more control, keeping the ball within reach. Mason smiled. "Better. Let's keep going."

They repeated the drill, and with each pass, Robin's touch became more delicate, more controlled. He started to feel the difference—how the ball responded to his feet, how a gentle touch made it easier to keep possession.

"Now let's work on dribbling," Mason said after a while, setting up cones in a line. "The goal is to keep the ball close to your feet as you move. Don't focus on speed— focus on control. The ball should always be within reach, no matter how fast or slow you're going."

Robin began weaving through the cones, but his touches were too heavy at first, and the ball kept getting away from him. Mason stopped him. "Smaller touches, Robin. The ball should be no more than a step away from you. Try to use both feet, alternating with each step."

Robin took a deep breath and started again. This time, he focused on keeping the ball close, using lighter, quicker touches with both feet. The difference was immediate. The ball stayed under control, and he could move through the cones more smoothly.

"Nice work," Mason said as Robin completed the drill. "That's the kind of control you need to keep defenders off you."

Next, Mason set up the turning drill. He positioned himself as a defender and had Robin receive the ball with his back to the goal. "In a game, you'll often be under pressure from defenders. You must turn quickly while maintaining control, especially when someone's right on you."

Mason sent the ball to Robin, who controlled it with his foot and attempted to turn, but it slipped away as Mason applied light pressure. "Use your body to shield the ball,"

Mason instructed. "When you turn, keep the ball close and use your body to protect it. Don't rush."

Robin tried again, using his body to block Mason from the ball as he turned. He felt more in control, able to spin quickly and maintain possession.

"Good. Keep practising that. The quicker you can turn while keeping control, the harder it'll be for defenders to take the ball."

After working on turning, Mason introduced a new drill: the juggling challenge. "This one's about your overall touch and control. You'll juggle the ball—keeping it in the air using your feet, thighs, and chest—but we're adding a twist. I'll call out different parts of your body, and you'll have to use that part to control the ball."

Robin raised an eyebrow, intrigued but nervous. "Juggling the ball is tough enough," he grinned.

Mason smiled. "That's the point. This drill helps you develop quick reflexes and soft touches with every part of your body. Ready?"

Robin nodded, and Mason started. "Foot!" he called as Robin began juggling the ball with his feet. "Thigh!" Robin popped the ball up with his thigh, focusing on keeping it steady. "Chest!" Robin brought the ball down, cushioning it with his chest before sending it back to his feet.

The drill was challenging but pushed Robin to improve his control with every touch. By the end of the session, Robin could juggle the ball smoothly, responding to Mason's calls and keeping the ball in the air with increasing confidence.

"That's the kind of control that sets you apart," Mason said, clapping Robin on the shoulder. "If you can master the ball in the air, you can control it anywhere."

The Ball Control Battle

Composure
Stay composed when the pressure mounts. With calm hands and a steady heart, you can handle any challenge.

The park was buzzing with energy as Robin arrived. The usual group of boys was already playing, and today, Robin felt a quiet confidence growing inside him. His touch was sharper, his dribbling tighter, and his ball control more precise. This wasn't just another game—this was his chance to test everything he'd learned with Mason.

"Robin, you're with us!" Jake called, motioning for Robin to join his team as he always did.

Robin jogged onto the field, feeling the ball at his feet, light and responsive. His hands flexed as he prepared to dive into the game, eager to see how his training would pay off.

On the opposing team stood Ethan, a boy Robin didn't know well but whose reputation on the field spoke for itself. Ethan was lean and quick, with sandy blond hair that fell into his sharp green eyes. He was known for his control and composure—always calm, always thinking ahead. Robin had noticed him in previous games, not for flashy moves, but for how effortlessly he could glide through defenders and set up plays with precision.

The game started quickly, and Robin didn't have to wait long to get involved. A high, lofted pass came, with Callum close on his heels. In the past, this would have been a moment of panic—trying to control a ball with a defender bearing down on him. But today, Robin was ready.

He watched the ball carefully, letting it drop just right. As it reached him, he cushioned it with the inside of his foot, trapping it gently and keeping it close. Callum lunged in, but Robin was already turning, using his body to shield the ball. With a quick touch, he spun away and passed the ball to Jake before Callum could recover.

"Nice touch, Robin!" Jake called as the play continued.

Robin smiled. That first touch had felt effortless, something that would have been tricky for him just a few weeks ago.

Ethan glanced over from his position on the wing, noticing the improvement in Robin's play. He said nothing, but the quiet nod he gave spoke volumes.

The game picked up in intensity, and soon Robin found himself dribbling down the sideline. Two defenders rushed at him, trying to box him in. Robin didn't panic. Instead, he slowed down, remembering Mason's advice about close control. Small touches, both feet, keep the ball close. He weaved between the defenders, the ball never more than a step away from him. One quick flick to the left, a dart to the right, and Robin was through, leaving the defenders behind.

The cheers from his teammates fueled him as he pushed forward. The ball felt like it was glued to his feet. Robin hadn't just beaten the defenders with speed—he'd done it with control.

As Robin continued his run, Ethan moved quickly to intercept, his long strides covering the ground swiftly. He was in front of Robin now, his eyes focused, ready for the challenge. Robin hesitated for just a moment, but then he remembered everything he had worked on. Quick touches, close control. He shifted to the right, then quickly cut to the left. Ethan's reaction was smooth, almost predicting the move, but Robin was faster this time. He darted past Ethan and passed the ball to Jake.

"Nice move," Ethan said, catching up as the play continued. There was a subtle smile on his face, one that acknowledged Robin's skill.

As the game went on, Robin's confidence continued to grow. He received a pass with his back to the goal, a defender pressing close behind him. It was the perfect opportunity to use the turning drills he had practised with Mason. Robin held the ball, felt the pressure from the defender, and used his body to shield it. With a quick spin, he turned sharply, keeping the ball close to his feet as he slipped away from the defender's grasp. The move was smooth, almost instinctive, and Robin was free to continue the play.

Then came the moment he had been waiting for—a one-on-one challenge with Callum. The two had often faced off, and Callum was the more formidable opponent. But today, Robin was ready. Callum charged in, his usual aggressive style on full display, but Robin kept his cool.

He used light, quick touches to keep the ball close, shifting from foot to foot as Callum tried to steal it. Every time Callum got close, Robin turned away, using his body to shield the ball and maintain control. Callum pressed harder, but Robin kept moving, his feet quick and his control flawless. With one final move, Robin faked a pass to the left, leaving Callum lunging in the wrong direction. Robin smoothly cut to the right, leaving Callum behind.

The crowd of boys erupted with cheers as Robin continued his run. Callum, visibly frustrated, could do nothing but watch as Robin raced toward the goal.

As the game wound down, Ethan caught up with Robin after another smooth play. "You've really been working on your control, haven't you?" he asked, glancing at Robin with genuine interest. "It shows."

Robin smiled, appreciating the acknowledgement. "Yeah, Mason's been helping me out. I didn't think it would make such a big difference at first, but it really has."

Ethan nodded, his green eyes flicking toward the ball. "Control is everything. Speed and strength—none of these matters if you can't control the ball. Keep at it. You've got something good going."

In the game's final moments, Robin received the ball just outside the box. His first touch was perfect, setting him up for the next move. He looked up and saw Jake making a run, and with one smooth pass, Robin set up the perfect assist. Jake took the shot, and the ball flew into the back of the net.

The game-winning goal.

Robin's teammates rushed over to him, clapping him on the back. "That was all you, Robin!" Jake shouted, beaming with excitement. "That control, that pass—it was perfect!"

Even Ethan, who was on the opposing team, gave Robin a nod of respect. "Well played," he said simply, but the weight of his words meant more to Robin than a dozen cheers.

Robin smiled, feeling the satisfaction of having earned respect, not just through speed or strength, but through control. Every touch, every turn, every movement had been deliberate, precise. His ball control had given him the edge, and it felt incredible.

As Robin walked off the field, soccer ball under his arm, he felt delighted. His training with Mason had paid off in ways he hadn't imagined. The ball was no longer something to chase—it was something he commanded. From now on, he knew that his touch and control would set him apart on the field, and his confidence in himself had never been stronger.

The Playmaker's Vision

Clarity

Creativity is the spark that changes the game. Trust your instincts and create something unforgettable.

The park felt the same as ever—kids kicking the ball, the chatter of teammates, and the faint breeze rustling through the trees. But for Robin, today felt different. He had been working on his touch, dribbling, and speed, but now Mason had promised to teach him something new. Something more advanced.

"Today, we're working on vision and awareness," Mason said as Robin approached. Robin raised an eyebrow, unsure of what that meant.

"It's not just about what's in front of you," Mason explained. "It's about seeing the entire field, reading the game, and knowing what will happen before it does. The best players who control the game don't just react—they anticipate."

Robin nodded, intrigued. He had seen the top players on TV always looking around, always seeming to know where the ball would go next. Now, it was his turn to learn that skill.

Mason started with a simple exercise. "I'm going to pass you the ball, but before you receive it, I want you to look up and call out the positions of two cones; imagine them as a player—either your teammates or opponents. This will teach you to keep your head up and constantly scan the field."

Robin positioned himself, ready for the pass. Mason played the ball toward him, and just before receiving it, Robin looked up, scanning the field. He quickly noticed Jake and Callum nearby. "Jake to my left, Callum to my right," Robin called, then trapped the ball with his foot.

"Good," Mason said with a nod. "But don't just stop there. Keep your head up every chance you get. You won't have much time to look around in a real game, so you have to do it constantly. Always be aware of where everyone is."

They repeated the drill several times, and each time, Robin became faster at scanning the field, calling out player positions before receiving the ball. At first, it felt strange—he was used to focusing on the ball. But as they went on, it became more natural. He realised how much more he could see when he lifted his head.

Next, Mason set up a more challenging drill. "Now, we're going to focus on reading the play. You will stand in one spot and track where your teammates and opponents are moving. I want you to call out where the space is opening up—where you think the ball should go."

Robin stood at the edge of the field as Mason and a few other players moved around, passing the ball between them. Robin observed, trying to predict where the play was heading. "The space is opening on the left!" he called out as Jake ran into an open area.

Mason nodded approvingly. "Exactly. It would be best if you watched for patterns in the game. Look for where the defenders are moving and where the gaps are opening. The more you do it, the more you'll see the game two or three steps ahead."

As the drill continued, Robin's vision became more apparent. He could see how players moved, how the defenders shifted to cover space, and where the opportunities would appear. It was like watching the game unfold in slow motion.

Finally, Mason set up the last drill of the day. "This is where vision and awareness count—decision-making under pressure. I will pass you the ball while defenders close in, and you'll have to decide whether to pass, dribble, or shoot quickly. But remember—keep your head up. Don't focus just on the ball; focus on what's happening around you."

Robin stood in the middle of the field, feeling the pressure mount as Mason played the ball to him. Callum and another defender closed in, but Robin didn't panic. He quickly glanced around—Jake was making a run into space. Robin quickly decided and passed the ball to Jake, who took off toward the goal.

"Great decision," Mason called out. "But you have to be able to do that faster. Let's go again."

They ran the drill several more times, and Robin's decisions became quicker each time. He started to see the game in a new way—anticipating where his teammates would be, knowing when the defenders were leaving space open, and choosing the right option faster.

By the end of the session, Robin felt a surge of confidence. He wasn't just reacting to the game anymore but reading it. He could see the whole field, not just the ball at his feet. And that made all the difference.

As they wrapped up, Mason clapped Robin on the shoulder. "You're starting to get it. Vision and awareness are what separate good players from great ones. It's about seeing the game from a higher level—anticipating, planning, and always being ready for what's next. Keep working on it, and you'll be one step ahead of everyone else."

Robin smiled, feeling a new sense of accomplishment. He knew that vision and awareness would take time, but today was a huge step forward. The game was becoming clearer to him, and he couldn't wait to put his new skills to the test in the next match.

Visionary Playmaking

Creativity
Creativity is the spark that changes the game. Trust your instincts and create something unforgettable.

Robin arrived at the park, his eyes scanning the familiar scene. The boys were already warming up, kicking the ball back and forth, but Robin's focus was different today. After all the training with Mason, he could feel a new sense of clarity. It wasn't just about controlling the ball or being fast—it was about seeing everything. Today, he would put his vision and awareness to the test.

Dylan, standing nearby, gave Robin a nod as he passed by. "Ready to play, Robin? Let's see what you've got today," Dylan said calmly, always composed on the field. His blue eyes scanned the field just like Robin's, but Robin felt the excitement bubbling inside him, knowing that today would be different.

As Robin joined the game, he could already sense the difference. His head stayed up, his eyes darting across the field, taking in where everyone was. Jake was pushing forward on the left, Callum hovered by the centre, and a gap was opening on the right side of the field. Robin could see the whole picture in a way he hadn't before.

The ball came to Robin at midfield, and instead of rushing to dribble forward, he quickly scanned the field. Jake was making a run down the left wing, and without hesitation, Robin sent a perfectly weighted pass into the open space. Jake sprinted after it, catching the defence off guard, and the play continued down the field.

"Great pass!" Jake called over his shoulder as he crossed the ball into the box. His voice carried a tone of surprise and admiration, showing how much he trusted Robin's vision now. Robin smiled, feeling the satisfaction of having seen the play develop before it even happened.

As the game continued, Robin found himself under pressure. Callum and Dylan closed in together, trying to trap him, but Robin didn't panic. Instead, he kept his head up, glancing around for options. To his right, one of his teammates was open. With a quick body shift, Robin sent the ball across before the defenders could close in.

"Nice try," Callum muttered, unable to hide his frustration as Robin slipped past his defence. Dylan, always calm, simply nodded in acknowledgement as he jogged back into position. "You're seeing the field better," Dylan commented, his blue eyes focused, clearly impressed by Robin's growing awareness.

Even under pressure, his ability to see the game kept his team in control.

Robin's confidence grew with every pass, every glance up to scan the field. He began anticipating where the defenders would move and could feel the game's rhythm flowing around him. During one critical moment, he noticed the defenders shifting to cover Jake, leaving space on the opposite side of the field. Without waiting, Robin adjusted his position and called for the ball.

When it came to him, Robin quickly sent a long pass into the open space, allowing his teammate to run onto it uncontested. The defenders scrambled to recover, but it was too late. His vision had opened up the play, giving his team a clear advantage.

"Good eye, Robin," Dylan called out from across the field, offering his approval in his usual understated way. He appreciated Robin's ability to spot those kinds of openings, the same kind of playmaking he often relied on as a defender.

Then came the moment Robin had been waiting for—a one-on-one with Callum. Callum charged at him, determined to steal the ball, but Robin kept calm. His head was up, observing Callum's movements. He could see the gap forming between Callum's legs as he lunged forward. With a quick feint, Robin slipped past him, keeping the ball close and easily dodging the tackle.

Callum stumbled, but Robin was already moving into open space, leaving him behind.

"I almost had you that time," Callum said, catching his breath but clearly impressed. He was competitive, but even he couldn't help but recognise Robin's ability to see the game unfold.

The final play of the game came quickly. Robin received the ball near the edge of the box, his eyes instantly scanning the field. The defenders were closing in fast, but he saw it—Jake was making an unmarked run into the penalty area. Without a second thought, Robin threaded the ball through the defence with perfect timing. Jake took one touch and fired it into the back of the net.

The final whistle blew. The game was over, and Robin's assist had sealed the victory.

Jake rushed over first, clapping Robin on the back. "That pass was brilliant, Robin! You saw the whole play before anyone else did!" he said with a huge grin, clearly thrilled with how Robin's awareness had led to the game-winning goal.

Dylan approached next, nodding in approval. "You're reading the game well now, Robin. You've got the vision we need out here." His words, though calm, carried weight—coming from Dylan, they were high praise.

Even Callum, though frustrated by being beaten again, walked over. He gave Robin a begrudging nod. "You see everything, don't you?" Callum muttered, unable to hide his respect. "Next time, I'll be ready."

Robin smiled. His vision and awareness have made a difference today. It wasn't just about reacting to what was in front of him anymore—it was about seeing the whole game unfold, reading the play, and making intelligent decisions faster than his opponents could.

As he walked off the field, soccer ball under his arm, Robin felt a deep pride. His ability to see the game had grown, and he knew it was becoming one of his greatest strengths. He was no longer just another player on the field—he could control the game's flow, anticipate what would happen next, and make the right decisions under pressure.

Robin's confidence soared as he realised how far he had come. He couldn't wait to see where his new skills would take him next.

Crossing the Line

Courage

To cross the line takes courage. Step beyond what you know and embrace the thrill of the unknown.

The field stretched out before Robin, and today, he knew he was about to take on a new challenge—crossing and long balls. He had worked on his vision, ball control, and speed, but now Mason wanted to show him how to send the ball across the field with accuracy and power.

Mason stood near the goalposts, waiting for Robin to join him. "Today, we're focusing on one of the most important skills for any player: crossing and long balls," Mason said. "These aren't just flashy moves—they're about delivering the ball where your teammates need it, not where you think it should go."

Robin nodded, understanding that precision was the key. He had seen countless games where a well-timed cross or long ball could change the entire momentum of a match. Now, it was his turn to learn how to make it happen.

"We'll start with crossing," Mason said, setting up a few cones in the box to simulate target areas. "When you're crossing, you need to think about the power, the angle, and the timing. A good cross can catch the defenders off guard, but it has to be accurate."

Mason demonstrated, driving a low cross toward the far post, where one of the cones stood as a marker. The ball whizzed past the imaginary defenders, landing perfectly in the target area. "See that? Low, driven, and fast. That's what you're aiming for."

Robin stepped up, positioning himself on the wing. He took a deep breath and struck the ball, aiming for the far post. The ball flew off his foot with power but soared too high, missing the target by a wide margin.

"Too much power," Mason said. "Keep it low and controlled. You want the ball to move quickly but not so fast that it overshoots everyone in the box."

Robin adjusted his approach, focusing on controlling the power of his cross. He took another shot, this time keeping it lower. The ball sailed through the air, landing closer to the target but slightly off.

"Better," Mason nodded. "Now, think about where your teammate is moving. It's not just about hitting the target—it's about timing. Watch their run and deliver the ball where they'll be, not where they are."

They practised several more crosses, and Robin's accuracy improved with each one. He began to feel the game's rhythm, watching where the space would open up and sending the ball into those gaps. His crosses became faster, more precise, and better timed.

After mastering the driven cross, Mason moved on to the next challenge—curving the ball. "When you bend the ball, it adds another layer of difficulty for defenders. They think they've got it covered, but then the ball curves away, straight to your teammate."

Mason demonstrated, curling the ball from the edge of the box, watching as it bent through the air and landed perfectly in the far corner. "Your turn," he said, smiling.

Robin tried his first curved cross, but the ball barely moved in the air, flying straight and missing the mark. "You need to hit it with the inside of your foot and follow through with a curve," Mason advised. "It's like drawing a line with your foot."

Robin gave it another try, this time focusing on the follow-through. The ball curved slightly, but it wasn't enough. He kept practising, adjusting his technique with each attempt. After several tries, Robin curled the ball perfectly, sending it into the box with a graceful arc.

"Now that's a cross!" Mason shouted, clapping his hands. "Keep practising that. The more you can bend the ball, the harder it'll be for defenders to stop."

Once Robin felt more confident with his crosses, they moved on to long balls. Mason explained how important long ball accuracy was, especially in transitioning from defence to attack. "A good long ball can change the entire flow of the game," he said. "But it needs to be accurate—

you don't want just to boot it down the field and hope for the best."

Mason set up cones at various distances and had Robin aim for them, focusing on precisely delivering the ball, not just power. At first, Robin struggled with balancing strength and accuracy. His long balls either needed to be more soft or overpowered, flying past the targets.

"Think about where your teammate will be, not just how far you can kick it," Mason said. "You need height to clear the defenders but accuracy to land it at your teammate's feet."

Robin adjusted his stance and focused on the timing of his strikes. He hit the ball with more control, watching as it sailed through the air and landed closer to the target. With practice, Robin's long ball delivery improved. He could now send the ball across the field with enough height to clear defenders but with the accuracy needed to find his teammates.

After several long ball drills, Mason set up a final challenge—crossing under pressure. "You won't have time to line up the perfect cross in a real game. Defenders will be closing you down. You must deliver the ball quickly, accurately, and under pressure."

Robin took his place on the wing as Mason played the role of a closing defender. With little time to think, Robin had to watch his teammates' movements and deliver the ball before Mason could block him. The pressure made it more complicated, pushing Robin to react faster. He timed his crosses better, hitting driven balls into the box even as Mason closed in.

By the end of the session, Robin felt more confident in his crossing and long-ball skills. He knew these were the kind of passes that could make the difference in a tight game.

The Ultimate Passing Test

Trust

Trust connects players and makes every pass possible.
Believe in your team, and the game will flow.

The sun was bright over the park as Robin stepped onto the field, feeling more prepared than ever. After the intense training with Mason, he knew that today's game would be the perfect opportunity to test his newly honed skills. Crossing and long balls—two techniques that could turn the tide of any game—were now part of his arsenal.

The game started quickly, and Robin was in midfield when the first opportunity came. He glanced up, spotting Jake running down the left wing, and instinctively knew what to do. Robin struck the ball in one smooth motion, sending it to sail high through the air. The long ball arced over the defenders, landing perfectly at Jake's feet. Jake took a touch, then fired a shot on goal, forcing the goalkeeper into a desperate save.

"Great ball, Robin!" Jake shouted as the play reset, his voice full of excitement. He gave Robin a quick thumbs up, clearly impressed by the precision of the pass. Robin smiled—his long ball had opened up the play, giving his team a real chance to score.

Robin was on the right wing a few minutes later, with defenders closing in fast. There wasn't much time to think—he needed to cross the ball before they could block him. He scanned the box, saw one of his teammates running toward the near post, and quickly whipped in a low, driven cross. The ball zipped past the defenders, landing exactly where he wanted it. His teammate met it with a powerful shot, but the goalkeeper blocked the ball.

Callum, who had been tracking back on defence, glanced over as the ball went out of play. "That was tight, Robin. You're really getting those crosses right on target today," he said, unable to hide a grudging respect.

Robin didn't mind. The cross had been spot on, and he knew another opportunity would come.

Midway through the game, Robin saw a chance to try something more challenging. The defenders had packed tightly into the box, making getting a straight cross-through difficult. This time, he decided to use the technique Mason had drilled into him—curling the ball around the defence. Robin struck the ball with his foot, watching as it bent beautifully through the air, curving toward the far post. One of his teammates leapt up to meet the cross, heading toward goal. The goalkeeper made a fingertip save, pushing the ball just over the bar.

"Unlucky!" Dylan called from across the field, his voice calm as usual. "That was a great cross, though," he added, jogging over to give Robin a quick nod of approval. Dylan appreciated precision, and Robin's curled cross had impressed him.

Robin felt a surge of pride. His ability to curl the ball around defenders had made the difference.

Later in the game, Robin's team was under pressure, defending deep in their half. The opposing team pushed hard and needed a way to relieve the pressure. Robin saw the opportunity. He took control of the ball, looked up, and sent a long ball high and wide into open space on the opposite side of the field. His teammates raced after it, catching the defence off guard and launching a counter-attack. The long ball had turned defence into offence in an instant.

Jake sprinted after the ball, catching up just before it rolled out of bounds. "Great vision, Robin!" he yelled over his shoulder, already setting up the next move. The long ball had shifted the momentum of the game, giving Robin's team the edge they needed.

As the clock ticked down, the score remained tied. Robin knew they needed something special to win the game. Then, the chance came. Robin found himself on the left wing, the ball at his feet, and Jake sprinting into the box. The timing was everything. Robin watched Jake's run, waited for the perfect moment, and then delivered a curling cross into the danger zone.

Jake rose above the defenders, his timing perfect, and met the ball with a powerful header. The goalkeeper dived, but he had no chance. The ball hit the back of the net, and the park erupted with cheers.

The game was over, and Robin's cross had sealed the win.

Jake was the first to reach Robin, clapping him on the back. "That was brilliant, Robin! You put it right where I needed it," he said, still catching his breath but grinning ear to ear. Robin could feel the genuine excitement in Jake's voice—it was a win they had earned together.

Dylan approached next, his blue eyes scanning the field as if replaying the game in his mind. "Solid passing today," he said quietly, giving Robin a thoughtful nod. "Your long balls are really opening up the game."

Even Callum, who had been competing fiercely all game, came over. He gave Robin a grudging nod. "Those crosses were spot on today," he muttered, clearly impressed despite his usual competitive edge. "You're making it hard for us to keep up."

Robin smiled, feeling the weight of his progress. His crossing and long ball skills had made a tangible impact on the game, and the respect from his teammates meant everything. He had turned practice into results, and his confidence had never been higher.

As he walked off the field, soccer ball under his arm, Robin knew that his ability to deliver under pressure had taken his game to a new level. Whether it was a perfectly timed cross or a long ball that shifted the game's momentum, he was now a player his teammates could rely on. And with friends like Jake, Dylan, and even Callum pushing him forward, Robin couldn't wait for the next challenge.

Set Pieces, Big Moments

Preparation
Big moments don't come by chance—they're earned through endless preparation. Be ready when it's your time.

The sun was dipping low as Robin and Mason stood near the edge of the field, the goal looming in the distance. Today was about mastering one of the most essential soccer skills—set pieces. The day's training focused on free kicks and corners, moments when a game could change instantly.

Mason stood by the ball, his eyes scanning the field. "Set pieces can win you games, Robin. They're all about precision, power, and placement. A good free kick or corner puts the ball exactly where it needs to be—not just anywhere. Today, we will ensure you can deliver when it matters most."

Robin nodded. He had seen enough games where a single free kick or corner decided the outcome. He wanted to be the player who could make that difference.

"We'll start with free kicks," Mason said, positioning the ball just outside the penalty area. "There are different ways to hit a free kick, depending on the situation. Sometimes, you want to curve the ball; other times, you'll want power. Let's start with bending it around the wall."

Mason stepped back and demonstrated the first free kick, striking the ball with his foot. The ball curved around the dummies set up as a wall, spinning into the top corner of the goal.

"Curving it like this is about creating spin," Mason explained. "You're using the inside of your foot to get that bend, making it hard for the goalkeeper to reach."

Robin took his place, eyeing the ball and the target ahead. He struck it, but the ball sailed straight, missing the target entirely.

"Too much power," Mason said. "You want to guide the ball with your foot, not just hit it. Try again."

Robin adjusted his stance, focusing on the technique Mason had shown him. This time, when he struck the ball, it curled slightly but still didn't have enough bend to reach the corner of the goal.

"It's better," Mason encouraged. "Keep working on it—focus on how you're striking the ball."

They repeated the drill several times, and Robin's ability to bend the ball improved with each attempt. After several tries, he managed to curve it around the wall and into the corner of the goal—the feeling of the ball hitting its mark filled Robin with a sense of achievement.

Next, Mason introduced him to the knuckleball free kick. "This one's tricky," Mason said. "It's all about hitting the ball with minimal spin, making it dip and swerve unpredictably. Goalkeepers hate it because they can't predict where it'll go."

Robin watched as Mason struck the ball cleanly with the knuckle of his foot. The ball flew straight at first, then dipped sharply, swerving just before hitting the back of the net.

Robin tried to replicate the technique, but his first few attempts flew wildly off course or had too much spin. It was more complicated than it looked.

"Keep your follow-through straight," Mason advised. "You want to hit the ball clean and let the lack of spin do the work."

After several more tries, Robin hit a knuckleball that dipped just as it reached the goal. It wasn't perfect, but it was progress, and Mason approved him.

After working on free kicks, they moved on to corner kicks. Mason explained the different types of corners Robin must deliver in a game. "A good corner can create chaos in the box," he said. "You can bend it toward the goal, away from the keeper or go low and fast to the near post. It all depends on what your team needs at the moment."

Robin took his place by the corner flag. His first attempt was an outswinger, bending the ball away from the goal. The ball flew too high, missing the mark entirely.

"Watch the height," Mason said. "You want it just over the defenders but low enough for your teammates to attack it."

Robin tried again, this time keeping the ball lower. It curled beautifully, dropping into the danger zone where Mason had placed cones to simulate his teammates. Robin could already picture how the defenders would struggle to deal with it.

Next, Mason had him practice the inswinger, curving the ball toward the goal. Mason explained that this type of corner was more dangerous because it could confuse the defenders and goalkeepers.

Robin hit the ball with his foot, watching it curl in, heading straight for the far post. The ball bent perfectly, landing in the exact spot Mason had pointed out.

"That's how you do it!" Mason cheered, clapping as Robin's confidence grew.

The last drill focused on near post delivery. Robin had to send the ball quickly and low to the near post, where a teammate could flick it on or score directly. Robin's first few attempts lacked the necessary speed, but with more practice, he got the hang of delivering a fast, dangerous cross that would catch defenders off guard.

By the end of the session, Robin was hitting free kicks with more accuracy and delivering corners with precision. Each set piece felt more natural, and he knew that in a game, these skills would be vital.

"You've come a long way, Robin," Mason said as they wrapped up. "Set pieces are pressure moments, but now you've got the tools to make something happen when it counts."

Robin smiled, feeling a new level of confidence. Free kicks and corners weren't just about the ball—they were about creating opportunities, changing the game, and making every moment count. He couldn't wait to test his new skills in the next match.

Taking the Free Kick

Confidence

Confidence is believing you can, even when the stakes are high. Take your shot and let your skill shine.

The park was buzzing with energy as Robin stepped onto the field. Today felt different. The work he'd put into mastering set pieces—free kicks and corners—was about to be tested in an actual match. Robin could feel the weight of the game, but he was ready. Every moment of practice with Mason had prepared him for this.

The first opportunity came sooner than Robin expected. Callum, consistently aggressive, had been fouled just outside the box, earning Robin's team a free kick. As Callum dusted himself off, he glanced at Robin. "This one's yours, Robin. Make it count," Callum muttered, walking back into position. Robin stepped forward as his teammates looked at him. This was his moment.

Standing in goal was Leo, the opposing team's new goalkeeper, known for his quick reflexes and sharp focus. Leo was taller than most of the other boys, with a lean build and sandy blond hair. His piercing green eyes tracked Robin as he lined up the free kick, and Leo positioned himself confidently, covering the middle of the goal but leaving just enough space in the top corner—challenging Robin to find it.

Robin placed the ball carefully, remembering Mason's advice—precision, power, and placement. The goalkeeper positioned himself near the centre of the goal, leaving a small gap in the far corner. Robin breathed deeply, visualising the ball curling around the wall and into that top corner.

He stepped up, striking the ball with the inside of his foot. It curled beautifully, bending around the wall. Leo dived to his left, stretching out his arms in a last-ditch effort, but it was too late—the ball sailed into the top corner, just as Robin had imagined.

The roar of his teammates filled his ears as they rushed over to congratulate him. "What a free kick!" Jake shouted, slapping Robin on the back. His face lit up with excitement. Robin grinned, feeling the rush of accomplishment. His training had paid off.

As the game continued, Robin's team won a corner kick. He jogged over to the flag, scanning the box. Dylan had positioned himself near the far post while Jake was ready for a quick run. Robin knew exactly what to do. He needed to deliver an inswinger—curved and dangerous.

Robin struck the ball with his foot, curling it toward the far post. Leo, now in goal, quickly reacted, his eyes locked on the ball as it sailed through the air. Dylan leapt into the air, meeting the ball with a powerful header, but Leo was quick on his feet and just managed to push the ball wide with his fingertips. Robin's teammates groaned in frustration, but Dylan gave him a nod of approval, saying, "Great cross, Robin. Keep those coming." Jake added a thumbs-up. "Next one's going in for sure."

The game was tight, and as the pressure mounted, Robin's team earned another free kick—this time deep in their half. It was a chance to relieve the pressure and push the game up the field. Robin stepped up again, this time aiming for distance.

He struck the ball cleanly, sending it high and wide into open space. His teammates sprinted forward, catching the opposing team off guard. Jake was the first to reach it, charging ahead and controlling the ball near the sideline. "Nice one, Robin! We needed that space," Jake shouted as the counter-attack launched. The long free-kick had shifted the game's momentum.

Then, with only minutes left and the score tied, Robin's team won a corner. It was their last chance to snatch a victory. Robin knew this had to be perfect.

He placed the ball, looked up, and saw Callum signalling for a run toward the near post. Robin delivered a fast, low cross without hesitation, aiming it where his teammate could flick it. The ball flew into the box, and his teammate reacted perfectly, glancing the ball with his head and sending it toward the net.

Leo sprang to life, diving toward the ball, but the speed and accuracy of the header were too much. Despite his effort, the ball slipped just past his outstretched hand and into the back of the net. The game was over. Robin's corner had delivered the winning goal.

The field erupted in cheers as his teammates swarmed him. "That was perfect, Robin!" Jake shouted, his face beaming with excitement. "You couldn't have placed it better!" Even Callum, though visibly frustrated by the loss, walked over with a grudging smile. "Your free kicks and corners are dangerous. You've stepped up."

Robin couldn't help but smile. The respect from his teammates and even Callum felt like validation for all the hard work he'd put in. His ability to take set pieces had become a real asset for the team, and he knew that these moments—these perfectly placed free kicks and corners—would be critical to future victories.

As Robin walked off the field, soccer ball under his arm, he felt more confident than ever. He had mastered one of the most challenging parts of the game, and his set pieces were no longer just practice—they were game-changing moments. Robin knew that, from now on, he could be the one to turn the tide of any match with a well-placed free kick or a perfectly timed corner.

Sportsmanship Above All

Respect

Respect for others makes you a true player. Show sportsmanship in every action, win or lose.

As Robin arrived, the sun hung low over the park, casting long shadows on the grass. There was something different in the air today, a sense of completion that filled him with pride and a touch of sadness. He had come so far since those first few sessions with Mason, and he knew this would be the last one.

Mason stood waiting by the edge of the field, a small smile on his face as Robin approached.

"You've done well, Robin," Mason began, his voice calm but filled with a hint of pride. "You've mastered all the technical skills I could teach you—dribbling, passing, shooting, defending, set pieces. But today, we will focus on something just as important, if not more."

Robin tilted his head, curious. "More important than the skills?"

Mason nodded. "Sportsmanship," he said. "It's the last lesson I can teach you. You see, soccer isn't just about being good with the ball. It's about being a good person on and off the field."

Robin listened carefully. This was something he hadn't expected. He remembered all the moments in his games—times when emotions ran high and competition had clouded his judgment. He realised Mason was right. The game wasn't about winning or losing and how you carried yourself.

"What do you mean by sportsmanship?" Robin asked, genuinely curious.

Mason leaned on the ball, his eyes meeting Robin's. "It means playing with respect—for your teammates, opponents, and the game itself. There's much emotion in soccer. You'll face tough situations, and tempers will flare, but a true player never lets that get in the way of respect. You win with grace, and you lose with humility."

Robin nodded slowly, absorbing the lesson. He had seen it himself—players who gloated after scoring or lashed out after losing. He knew what kind of player he wanted to be.

"But what if someone's being unfair?" Robin asked. "What if they're playing dirty or not showing respect themselves?"

Mason smiled softly as though he had expected the question. "It's easy to get caught up in what others are doing wrong. But here's the thing, Robin—sportsmanship isn't about how others act. It's about how you respond. You can't control their behaviour, but you can always control yours."

He continued, his voice steady. "When someone plays dirty or shows disrespect, it's your job to rise above it. Stay focused, stay calm, and, most importantly, stay respectful. That's what separates great players from the rest."

Robin thought about Callum, his rival in so many games. Callum was aggressive, competitive, and sometimes even harsh. But Robin had noticed something lately—his responses to Callum had changed. He no longer felt the need to prove anything to him. Instead, he focused on his game, letting his skills and actions speak for themselves.

"I think I understand," Robin said slowly. "It's about respecting everyone, no matter what happens in the game."

Mason nodded. "Exactly. And remember, you'll be remembered not just for your skills but for how you treated others. Your teammates will look up to you, your opponents will respect you, and the game will reward you."

Robin glanced at the field, feeling a sense of closure. "So... this is the last lesson?"

Mason smiled, the look of a mentor proud of his student. "It's the last lesson I can give you, Robin. The rest is up to you. You've got the skills and the mindset, and now you've understood what it means to be a true player. Soccer is about more than just kicking a ball. It's about how you carry yourself through every match, every challenge."

Robin was quiet for a moment, then looked up at Mason. "Thank you. For everything. I wouldn't be where I am without your help."

Mason's smile widened. "It's been a pleasure watching you grow, Robin. But remember, this journey doesn't end here. Keep working, keep pushing yourself, and always respect the game and the people around you. That's what makes a player truly great."

Robin nodded, his heart filled with gratitude. He realised this was more than just a lesson in soccer—it was a life lesson. Sportsmanship, respect, and humility would stay with him long after the matches ended.

Robin kicked the ball gently as the sun dipped lower, reflecting on his journey. He had learned so much, not just about soccer, but about himself. Mason had given him the tools to succeed, but the values of respect and sportsmanship would guide him through the rest of his journey.

As they parted ways, Mason gave Robin one final piece of advice. "Remember, Robin, soccer is a game, but respect is forever. Be the player who lifts others, treats everyone with kindness, and plays the game correctly."

Robin smiled. "I will, Mason. I promise."

Robin walked off the field, the ball under his arm, knowing this was just the beginning. He had all the skills he needed, but more importantly, he had learned what it truly meant to be a player—not just in soccer, but in life.

The Ultimate Test

Perseverance
Perseverance is the strength to push forward, even when it's tough. Stay strong—you're almost there.

The day was perfect for soccer. The sun shone brightly over the park, and Robin could feel the energy in the air. Today's match wasn't just another game—it was a chance for him to show everything he had learned. Mason's teachings had prepared him for this moment, and he was ready.

As the game began, Robin quickly took control. The ball moved smoothly at his feet, and his every decision was sharp. Jake darted ahead on the left wing, calling for the ball. "Robin, over here!" Robin glanced up and sent a perfectly timed pass into Jake's path. His speed and agility allowed him to break through the defenders, and his vision was sharper than ever, setting up his teammates for chance after chance.

Midway through the first half, Robin found himself with the ball near the edge of the box. He knew what to do. He stepped up and curled a beautiful shot into the top corner of the net, leaving the goalkeeper helpless. Leo, in goal, dived but couldn't reach it in time. His teammates cheered, but Robin stayed focused. There was more to come.

The game continued, and Robin's skills shone brightly. He defended confidently, blocking attackers and reading the game like never before. Dylan, positioned defensively, called out, "Watch the right side, Robin!" as the opposing team pressed forward. Robin nodded, tracking the ball and intercepting a pass before it could cause danger. His ball control kept possession even under pressure, and every time he delivered a long ball or a cross, it created a new opportunity for his team.

Then came the moment he'd been waiting for—his team won a free kick just outside the box. Without hesitation, Robin stepped forward, the ball at his feet. Callum, standing nearby, gave him a nod. "This is your moment, Robin. Show them what you've got." Robin glanced at the goalkeeper, who positioned himself nervously. Robin took a deep breath, then struck the ball cleanly, bending it around the wall and into the top corner. Leo dived again but could only watch as the ball curled beyond his reach.

His teammates erupted in celebration, and Robin smiled, knowing that all the hours of practice had paid off.

As the game went on, Robin's leadership became even more apparent. Jake ran up alongside him, grinning. "Lead the way, Robin. You're running the show out here," he said, clapping Robin on the back. His teammates looked to him for guidance, and he controlled the match's pace. His corner kicks were perfect, delivering dangerous balls into the box, leading to more goals. Everything was falling into place.

Then, something unexpected happened. A group of new kids appeared at the edge of the field, watching the game with wide eyes. After a few minutes, one of them gathered the courage to step forward. "Can we play too?" he asked, his voice nervous but hopeful.

Robin's teammates exchanged glances. "They don't look that good," Callum muttered, crossing his arms. "They'll slow us down."

Robin stepped forward, smiling at the new kids. "Of course, you can play," he said warmly. "It doesn't matter how good you are. What matters is that you want to play soccer. That's all that counts."

His teammates looked surprised, but Robin's calm leadership set the tone. Jake glanced at Robin, then shrugged. "Alright, let's give them a chance," he said with a grin. Even Dylan, who was usually quiet, nodded in agreement. "Everyone starts somewhere," he said, adding his support.

The new kids joined the game, and at first, they struggled. They missed passes, fumbled the ball, and couldn't keep up with the match's pace. But Robin encouraged them at every turn. He slowed the game down when needed, making sure they were involved.

"You've got this!" Robin called to one of the new players as they tried to control the ball. He passed to them, called out their names, and gave them space to play.

"Don't worry about mistakes," Robin said with a smile. "Just enjoy the game. That's what it's all about."

The atmosphere of the match began to change. Callum, who had been sceptical at first, started passing to the new players, too, giving them opportunities to contribute. "Keep going; you're doing great," he said to one of them after a pass. The new kids started to relax, and their confidence grew. Inspired by Robin's attitude, his teammates began to embrace the new players as well, including them in the game's flow. Slowly but surely, the game became less about winning and more about enjoying the experience together.

Robin looked around the field as the game drew close, feeling proud. Leo, who had been keeping the goal solidly throughout the match, called out, "You've really brought everyone together today, Robin. This is how soccer should be." Robin had used everything Mason taught him—his skills, vision, and leadership. But more than anything, he had learned the true meaning of soccer: it wasn't just about how good you were. It was about the love of the game and the joy of playing with others.

When the final whistle blew, the new kids left the field smiling, feeling like they belonged. Robin's teammates came over, patting him on the back.

"You are the best, Robin," Jake said, smiling. "Not just because of how you play, but because of how you treat everyone."

Dylan walked up next, nodding thoughtfully. "You showed us that soccer's about more than just winning. It's about everyone enjoying the game," he said, his usual calm demeanour carrying extra weight. Even Callum, who had been competitive throughout, gave Robin a small smile. "You were right, Robin. It's not about being the best, but making sure everyone gets to play."

Robin grinned. "It's not about being the best," he replied. "It's about playing the game and making sure everyone enjoys it. That's what matters."

As Robin walked off the field, soccer ball under his arm, he felt a deep pride. He had shown that soccer was more than just skills—it was about respect, inclusion, and having fun. At that moment, Robin knew he had become the player and the person Mason had always believed he could be.

A New Beginning

Hope
Every ending is a fresh start. Embrace new beginnings with hope, for they hold endless possibilities.

It was an ordinary day at the park. The sun cast its usual warm glow over the field, and the familiar group of kids gathered to play their daily soccer game. Robin was there, of course—just as he had been daily. The new kids he had welcomed into the game were also eager to get started. It felt like any other day, but today would be different.

Robin played like he always did, using everything he had learned from Mason. His dribbling was sharp, his passes perfectly timed, and his defence solid. Every move he made on the field felt effortless, a testament to the hours of practice and dedication. He no longer had to think about each action—his body knew what to do.

As the game progressed, Robin took control, leading his team with quiet confidence. After weaving through defenders, he scored a beautiful goal and set up another with a perfectly curled cross from the wing. His teammates relied on him to guide the play, and Robin was happy to rise to the challenge.

But what Robin didn't know was that someone had been watching. From the sidelines, a coach from the local soccer team observed every move he made. The coach had seen Robin play before, but today was different—Robin wasn't just the best player on the field; he was a leader who made everyone around him better.

When the game ended and the kids started to pack up, the coach approached Robin. He wore a serious but friendly expression, his eyes full of admiration for the young player.

"Robin," the coach called out.

Robin turned, surprised to see the coach walking toward him. "Yes?" he asked, wiping the sweat from his brow.

"I've been watching you for a while now," the coach said, smiling. "You've got real talent, both with your skills and how you carry yourself on the field. We need players like you on our team. How would you feel about joining us?"

Robin blinked, taken aback. "Me? Really?"

The coach chuckled. "Yes. You've got what it takes, Robin. And it's not just about your technical ability—it's about how you lead and respect the game. That's what makes you stand out."

Robin felt a wave of excitement wash over him. The idea of joining a real team, of taking his love for soccer to the next level, was something he hadn't even considered. Yet here it was, right in front of him.

"I'd love to join," Robin said, his voice filled with gratitude. "Thank you."

The coach nodded. "We'll be in touch soon. I'm excited to see what you can do."

As the coach walked away, Robin stood momentarily, letting the news sink in. He glanced over at his teammates, who were still discussing the game, completely unaware of what had happened. His heart swelled with pride.

As Robin walked off the field, soccer under his arm, he remembered everything Mason had taught him. He had started this journey unsure of his skills, struggling to fit in, but now he was stronger, both on and off the field. The lessons of respect, sportsmanship, and passion for the game had shaped him into the player he had become.

Robin smiled, knowing that a new one was beginning while this chapter of his journey was closing. The future was wide open, and he was ready for whatever came next.

He realised soccer wasn't just about winning or being the best. It was about the journey—the lessons learned, the people you meet, and the love you develop for the game. Robin had found that love and was ready to share it.

THE END

until the next challange
begins...

Afterword

Dear Readers,

Thank you for joining me on this journey through the game of soccer and beyond. Soccer isn't just a sport; it's a way of learning about life. In every pass, every tackle, and every moment of teamwork, soccer teaches us values that go far beyond the field.

When you step onto the field, you're doing more than just playing a game—you're practising determination, learning to communicate, and showing respect for others. Soccer requires focus, resilience, and the courage to keep pushing forward, even when the outcome is uncertain. These same qualities matter in life. Whether you're facing a difficult moment, working toward a goal, or finding your place in a team, the lessons from soccer stay with you.

Like in soccer, real life has its own challenges, setbacks, and moments of triumph. Sometimes, you're the one scoring the goal, and other times, you're supporting your teammates so they can shine. Soccer reminds us that everyone has a role to play, and each role matters. It's not about being the best; it's about doing your best, respecting others, and never giving up.

Through this book, I hope you see how the skills and values learned in soccer can be the building blocks of good character. Every game is a chance to grow, not just as a player but as a person. I encourage you to take what you've learned here onto the field and into the world beyond it.

Remember, soccer is more than just a game. It's a journey of learning, growing, and becoming the best version of yourself. Enjoy the journey, and play with heart.

Toby Rivers

ON THE
PITCH
MASTERING THE SKILLS
BY
TOBY RIVERS

ON THE
PITCH
MASTERING THE POSITIONS
BY
TOBY RIVERS

ON THE
PITCH
MASTERING THE DEFENCE
TOBY RIVERS

Made in the USA
Las Vegas, NV
21 May 2025